**SOON TO BE A MAJOR
MOTION PICTURE**

Other books by Donna Partow

SOON TO BE A MAJOR MOTION PICTURE

New Direction for Life's Dramas

DONNA PARTOW

Revell
Grand Rapids, Michigan

Published by Fleming H. Revell
a division of Baker Publishing Group
P.O. Box 6287, Grand Rapids, MI 49516-6287

Second printing, June 2005

Printed in the United States of America

Library of Congress Cataloging-in-Publication Data
Partow, Donna
    Soon to be a major motion picture: new direction for life's dramas / Donna Partow.
        p.   cm.
    Includes bibliographical references.
    ISBN 0-8007-3071-2 (pbk.)
    1. Christian women—Religious life. I. Title.
    BV4527.P376 2005
    248.8′43—dc22   2005001691

First Generation Christian is a trademark of Donna Partow (filing in process).

Contents

Acknowledgments

My heartfelt gratitude to the women who contributed to this book, The Major Motion Picture Yahoo Group members:

Jeanine Barrett
Wendy Bartley
Vicki Bedford
Colleen Bell
Darsi Brinley
Chrissy Company
Betty Culley
Julie Anne Custer
Terri Fields
Lynne Ford
Kim Frisbee
Virginia Garrett
Cindy Hannon
Denise Isaac

Rebecca Johnson
Renee Kroll
Shirley Lind
Judy Lovitt
Gayle Lowery
Eve Maxwell
Audrey Outhouse
Amy Ridgeway
Connie Schmoll
Gwen Scott
Margaret Scovell
Kim Serban
Judy Sheridan
Michelle Waters

Introduction

Are Your Problems Making You Crazy?

My husband is driving me crazy!

My kids are making me batty!

My boss is driving me up the wall!

This church is enough to try the patience of a saint!

If one more person asks me to do one more thing, I'm going to lose my mind!

Is any of this sounding slightly familiar??? Of course, you've never said any of those things, but you have a distant cousin in another state . . .

What's that? You've uttered every one of those lines in the last week? I can relate. Many authors conduct extensive research before writing a book. Alas, no research was required for this one. All I had to do was write the truth about my own life and voila: the raw material for a future Major Motion Picture was born.

I used to think my problems were making me crazy. But then I realized I had it backward: my craziness was making the problems! For reasons we shall soon explore, like many women I tended to blow my problems all out of proportion. I could turn the slightest inconvenience, like losing my car keys, into an ordeal. If someone so much as hurt my feelings, I expected Oliver Stone to turn up at any moment, demanding the story rights.

My three favorite pastimes were:

1. Thinking about how awful my life was
2. Telling everyone who got within a mile of me how awful my life had been
3. Wondering why I didn't have any friends

If those are among your favorite pastimes, too, God has provided a way of escape: putting your problems into perspective. Here's how the Bible puts it:

> Pursue the things over which Christ presides. Don't shuffle along, eyes to the ground, absorbed with the things right in front of you. Look up, and be alert to what is going on around Christ—that's where the action is. See things from his perspective.
>
> Colossians 3:1–2 Message

Perspective is a powerful thing. As Rick Warren put it: "Your perspective will influence how you invest your time, spend your money, use your talents and value your relationships."[1] According to the dictionary, perspective is (1) "the capacity to view things in their true relations or relative importance," or (2) "the art of giving due diminution to the strength of light, shade and colors of objects, according to their distances and the quantity of light falling on them, and to the medium through which they are seen." That's what I hope to provide in this book:

an opportunity to turn your Major Motion Picture into something beautiful by putting some distance between you and your problems. I hope this book enables you to take a step back and look at your life from a different point of view. You may even realize that your situation is not quite so black-and-white as you originally thought. But the real key is found in shedding the light of God's truth upon your life.

As Christians, we know God is a Redeemer. That's another way of saying he can take a worthless situation and create something good out of it. Sometimes it takes a while, though. Nearly a decade ago, a friend and I drove three hours (round-trip) to visit a living history museum. Can I be honest? It was so boring we both felt we'd wasted our time and money. Until last year, when I realized that trip was priceless. God had planted a seed of truth in my heart that day, but it took years of watering and quiet cultivation before it finally saw the light of day. Let me tell you, when it finally broke through, I was singing the "Hallelujah Chorus."

Now about that seed. My friend and I were apparently the only people touring the history museum that day, but being good sports, the staff decided to proceed with "the show" anyway. So there we sat, the only audience members, when a young man came out from behind the curtain and announced that their small troupe of performers was about to recreate an authentic nineteenth-century art form called the melodrama. As the show proceeded, I remember feeling embarrassed for the actors and actresses, since the play was absolutely preposterous.

I should have been embarrassed by my ignorance, because they had, indeed, accurately recreated a nineteenth-century melodrama. What exactly is a melodrama? The phrase originates from the words *music drama* because music was used to accentuate the already over-the-top

11

actions and emotions of the actors and actresses. Every character was one-dimensional: the villain was entirely villainous; the heroine was a powerless victim awaiting rescue; and the hero, who arrived just in the nick of time, was entirely good. Everything was black-and-white. No shades of gray, let alone various colors of the rainbow.

As I began to ponder this lost art form, a voice whispered in my ear, "Does that sound like anyone you know, Donna?"

Let's see: a one-dimensional universe featuring an entirely villainous villain and a powerless victim awaiting rescue by the perfect man.

Uh-oh.

The still, small voice continued: "Remember how ridiculous you thought the actors in the play looked?"

Yes, I remembered.

"That's how *you* look, child. All the world is *not* your personal stage and you are *not* a player upon it. You've wasted enough years on your melodramas. Come, follow me, and I will give you rest for your weary soul."

You will search the Bible in vain for melodrama. I know. I've looked. It's not in there. God's not into melodrama. He's into honesty and reality. That's why every character on every page is portrayed in a multidimensional fashion, faults and all. Over and over again, God clearly shows us that *in almost every single case*, people played a role—however small—in creating their own problems. We'll be looking at such real-life examples throughout *Soon to Be a Major Motion Picture*, in hopes that we will discover that maybe, just maybe, we too have played a small role in creating our own problems. Our best hope for a brighter future is in learning how to turn our melodramas into "mellow dramas."

It's my earnest prayer that this book will enable you to gain a broader perspective on your own life and your place in this world. I want you to discover what I've discovered by God's grace: that it really *is* possible to respond to your problems with calm and confidence, rather than reacting as if every moment is a major drama. Yes, it's true other people have contributed to your problems, too. Yes, there are reasons why you are the way you are, but you *can* change. And only *you* can make those changes. You are not a performer on a grand stage called Planet Earth, nor are you a paid actress in a prescribed script with no choice but to play out the destiny determined in advance for you. You're not a helpless victim of circumstances. You are a human being, made in the image of Almighty God. You are capable of rising above *anything* that comes your way by the transforming power of his Holy Spirit at work within you.

The Porcupine State of Mind

Last year, I was invited to speak at Sandy Cove Conference Center in North East, Maryland. Since their facility is within driving distance of my family in New Jersey, I thought, *You know, Donna, why not fly in early? Spend some quality time with your family and impart to them the joy of the Lord.*

You can probably already guess I was heading for trouble long before I had my boarding pass in hand.

I arrived at my sister's house, and within an hour we got into a ridiculous debate about something that had happened when I was in eighth grade. The disagreement centered around one particular incident, but for me it symbolized something greater. It wasn't just that this person had hurt me one time. I wasn't talking about a one-time disappointment—the kind of thing you can eventually get past. This person *routinely* hurt me. It was, for me, a disappointing relationship. There's a huge difference between a disappoint-*ment* and disappoint-*ing*. It's the "ing" that gets you. Have you ever experienced that? Just when you think you've forgiven that person (or group of people), they do something *else* to hurt you. The pain never seems to end no matter how hard you try.

That's why I wanted my sister to acknowledge my right to feel hurt by my relationship with this particular person. Instead, we just went round and round. My sister and I are best friends. We rarely fight about anything, but we were ready to tear each other's heads off.

Now, this next bit is the most important part of the story, so I don't want you to lose sight of it. If you miss it, you'll miss my whole point: *I was right.*

I was right and, furthermore, my sister was wrong. Let's face it: I think I know a little better than she does what happened *in my life*. I think I can tell when someone isn't treating me right.

Well, so much for the joy of the Lord! I was in such a state of mind, you can't even imagine it. Well, okay, you've probably been there many times yourself. I could not think of anything else except: I was right and she was wrong. I couldn't read my Bible. Couldn't pray. Couldn't even think straight. This one topic and this topic only consumed my every waking moment: I was right; she was wrong. My mind was filled with all the *good points* I could marshal to prove my case. I spent day and night rehearsing the sermon of the century, which I would deliver to her someday when I had both the courage and the opportunity. Then she would finally have to admit what I knew to be true: I was right and she was wrong.

In short, I was an emotional wreck. Over something that had happened twenty-eight years ago. Why? Because I had been wronged. And because my sister refused to acknowledge just how wronged I had been. It was vitally important for her to acknowledge that I had been wronged, because how else could she see how God had helped me rise above it all until she acknowledged just how low I had been!?!

Am I scaring you? Or maybe even reminding you how melodramatic you can be sometimes?

Well, after two miserable days, my precious father agreed to drive me, spiritual leader that I am, down to Maryland so I could impart deep spiritual truths to my fellow human beings. As I stepped onto the elevator, I couldn't miss the poster with my picture on it. The one that described my upcoming spiritually uplifting, life-changing seminar. Just then, the Lord spaketh unto me. Guess what he said? He said: "Who cares? You're right; she's wrong. Look how far being right has gotten you. You're nothing but a porcupine! It was twenty-eight years ago. Let it go already."

A porcupine? I thought to myself. *Did God just call me a porcupine?*

Do you know what a porcupine is? It's a creature with a lot of good points, but nobody wants to be around it. The world is just filled with porcupines; so is the church. A porcupine is a woman with a lot of good points, but nobody wants to be around her. She is absolutely right. And if the people in her life would just listen to her and get with the program, she knows the world would be a much better place. Given half a chance, she could easily straighten out her husband, her kids, her church, you name it. Yet, strangely enough, nobody wants to hear it from her. I wonder why that is.

A porcupine is a woman with a lot of good points, but nobody wants to be around her.

17

Have you, by any chance, noticed that despite your vast storehouse of wisdom and insight, people aren't exactly flocking to you for counsel? You may keep busy—in fact, you may even create a frenzy of activity to mask your loneliness. But I'm not talking about running around like a crazy woman. I mean do people seek a deep, personal relationship with you? Are they eager to know the *real you*, to listen to your heart and share their deepest concerns with you? Or do people keep you at arm's length?

Let me give you a few examples:

- If you are a loving, thoughtful friend, but you can never find anyone to be a true friend in return, it could be that you have the misfortune of living in the one town on the planet that is completely devoid of nice people . . . or you could be a porcupine.
- If you are the best neighbor anyone could wish for, yet your neighbors never invite you over, it could be that they are rude and inconsiderate . . . or you could be a porcupine.
- If you are the hardest worker at your place of employment; if you are single-handedly running the company, yet you keep getting passed over for promotions, it could be that your boss is blind to your contributions or envious of your talent . . . or you could be a porcupine.
- If you are more eager to serve God than anyone else is at your church, and you know the Bible inside out and backward and routinely have "a word from the Lord," yet you are not called upon, it could be that your spiritual leaders are out of touch with God . . . or you could be a porcupine.
- If you devoted your entire life to your children, but for some reason your grown children (and grand-

18

children) don't come around unless they have to, it could be that they are selfish and thoughtless . . . or you could be a porcupine.

- If you are an amazing wife, but your husband doesn't appreciate you at all . . . you could be a porcupine. In fact, there are so many porcupine wives that we're going to devote an entire chapter to the subject!
- If you love God but your life is a mess, it could be that the enemy[1] is out to get you . . . or you could be a porcupine.

Just one more clue to help you determine whether or not you may be a porcupine: if you routinely deliver silent sermons in your head, you are most definitely a porcupine! To be honest, I used to deliver a hundred silent sermons a day, to everyone from store clerks to my pastor. I was always rehearsing all my good points in preparation for the big moment when I would rise up and set the world straight.

I shared the Seventeenth-Century Nun's Prayer[2] in my previous book *Becoming a Vessel God Can Use*, and I often read it aloud at my conferences. But it's so good I think it bears repeating.

> Lord, you know better than I know myself that I am growing older and will someday be old.
> Keep me from the fatal habit of thinking I must say something on every subject and on every occasion.
> Release me from the craving to straighten out everybody's affairs. Make me thoughtful, but not moody.
> Helpful, but not bossy.
> With my vast store of wisdom, it seems a pity not to use it all,
> but you know, Lord, that I want a few friends at the end.

19

Keep my mind free from the endless recital of details;
   give me wings to get to the point.
Seal my lips on my aches and pains.
They are increasing, and love of rehearsing them is
   becoming sweeter as the years go by.
I dare not ask for grace enough to enjoy the tales of
   others' pains, but help me to endure them with
   patience.

I dare not ask for improved memory, but for a growing humility and a lessening cocksureness when
   my memory seems to clash with the memories of
   others.
Teach me the glorious lesson that occasionally—I may
   be mistaken.

Keep me reasonably sweet.
I do not want to be a saint—some of them are so hard
   to live with. But a sour old person is one of the
   crowning works of the Enemy.
Give me the ability to see good things in unexpected
   places, and talents in unexpected people.
And give me, Lord, the grace to tell them so.

Amen

If a frightening number of those "you could be a porcupine" scenarios rang true for you, I would urge you
to make the Seventeenth-Century Nun's Prayer your
prayer. It's not enough just to read it through once. You
need to pray it aloud. Write it out in your prayer journal,
over and over again. Meditate on it daily. Let its message seep down into your soul and change your way of
thinking. Romans 12:18 says, "If it is possible, as far as
it depends on you, live at peace with everyone." It's up
to you, friends. Do you want to be right? Or do you want
to live in peace? Take it from a recovering porcupine:
being right is way overrated.

Let me tell you a revolutionary truth. Few things matter less in this life than who's right and who's wrong. It just flat-out doesn't matter. Yet how many of us devote an inordinate amount of time, energy, and phone conversations to that very subject? I know women who talk about *nothing else*. I urge you to think about what you are thinking about, and listen to the subjects you talk about. If you are fixated on who's right and who's wrong, you've got a problem. The Bible says:

> If you are fixated on who's right and who's wrong, you've got a problem.

Fix your thoughts on Jesus.

Hebrews 3:1

Let us fix our eyes on Jesus, the author and perfecter of our faith, who for the joy set before him endured the cross, scorning its shame, and sat down at the right hand of the throne of God. Consider him who endured such opposition from sinful men, so that you will not grow weary and lose heart.

Hebrews 12:2–3

Fix these words of mine in your hearts and minds; tie them as symbols on your hands and bind them on your foreheads.

Deuteronomy 11:18

Fix your eyes on Jesus and stop trying to fix people! Repeat: it does NOT matter who's right and who's wrong. This is not a melodrama in which someone has to be the villainous villain so you can be the innocent heroine. What matters is who's willing to repent and who's willing to forgive. In point of fact, being right can be very dangerous to your soul. Because being right is such a comfortable place. You can just sit yourself right down and refuse to go anywhere else. You are right and you shall not, you shall not be moved.

Listen to me: If there's one thing I have learned from ministering to women around the world, it's this: *What trips up most Christians is not our own sin, but our sinful response to the sin of others.*

I'm completely in earnest when I say our sin, honest-to-goodness, is not the problem. In fact, we are not the problem. *They* are the problem. (We all know who *they* are!) We are nice church ladies. We're not drug addicts. We're not alcoholics. We don't have a gambling problem. We're not even addicted to soap operas anymore . . . except . . . well. Okay, next subject. We're not floozies hanging out in bars. We're not surfing Internet porn sites.

If I've said it once, I'll say it a million times: We are not the problem. They are the problem. And *that's* the problem. Because when you are not the problem, and you know perfectly well that *you* are right and the other person is wrong, you are drowning, but no one's going to come rescue you.

If you are drinking, or gambling, or doing drugs, or sleeping around, eventually one of your fellow Christians will pick up the phone or stop by your house and say, "You really shouldn't be doing that." But if you're just a church lady trapped in the Porcupine State of Mind, chances are no one will ever say a word. Not to your face anyway. Truth be told, you'll probably blend right in at your local church, where you can sit around and swap stories with other miserable women with lousy husbands, ungrateful kids, and thankless friends. You can take turns fashioning the scripts of your very own Major Motion Picture in which you star as the most ill-treated, unappreciated person in the history of human civilization. And you can sit in the pew forever and never find the hope and healing you need just as desperately as the woman who's living in flagrant sin. Sad to say, she's often more likely to get the help she needs than you are—except that now you've picked up this book.

I often tell the story of a divorced woman I met at a Christian conference some years ago. Her husband was chronically unfaithful and eventually left her for another woman. She was clearly right; her husband was clearly wrong. She stood before me, her whole body trembling, as she shared some of the cruel things this man had done. My heart just broke for her. But as more details began to unfold, I realized something wasn't quite adding up. I had assumed this man had just walked out on her a month ago; the wound seemed so fresh. So I asked her, "How long ago did your husband leave?"

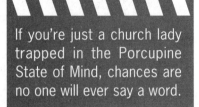

If you're just a church lady trapped in the Porcupine State of Mind, chances are no one will ever say a word.

"Twenty-two years ago," she said.

I just about fell on the floor.

She didn't sign up for a painful marriage. Certainly didn't sign up for divorce. But until she forgives her former husband, she is signing up daily to let the enemy have a field day with her life. It's interesting to note that not only was her health a wreck, but she said her grown children were having health and relationship problems. I mean Major Motion Picture–sized problems.

But she was right. And how far did that get her? Not very far.

The church will deal with outward sins of behavior, but it is the inward attitude of the heart that God cares about. Believe me when I tell you, because I know from personal experience, that your sinful response to the sin of others is often more defiling and more damaging than the sin that was originally committed against you. It is the inward sins of the heart that drain the life from our souls.

Here's the hard, cold truth we'll be facing throughout the pages of this book: we all endure tough times. It is inevitable. But it's not what happens to us that determines the type of people we become; it's how we respond to what happens to us. Your husband, your kids, your boss, your church—they are not your problem. They may have a truckload of problems, but those are their problems. Your problem is how you are responding to their problems. Do you want to smack me for saying that or what? Go ahead and swing away. But I promise what I've just said is true.

That divorced woman had a lot of great points. She had every right to be devastated by the collapse of her marriage; but she also has a right to hope and healing. Unfortunately, she can't have both. At some point, she'll have to let go of the need to be right and start pursuing the need to be healed. At some point, she'll have to put her pain into perspective, realizing she's not the first woman to be betrayed by a man, and she certainly won't be the last. I know, because that's the point I finally had to reach in my own life.

I have a picture that was taken of me on May 4, 1999, and someday I'll have the courage to include it for all the world to see on my website. But I'm not there yet. If you saw that photo, you would conclude that I was a fiftysomething woman dying of a terminal disease. Now, there's nothing wrong with looking like you're fifty when you're sixty. But I was in my thirties. By the way, I did have a terminal disease at the time. It was bitterness. And was it killing me!

I was such an expert on everyone else's sins. Over and over, I pointed out to God how everyone had done me wrong. Then finally he held the mirror of truth before me and said, "My child, I know all about it. But I am afraid for you. Look at the woman in this mirror."

I was right; everyone else was wrong. At least, that's my story and I'm sticking to it. So why was I the one who looked—and felt—like I was dying? You have probably heard this before, but I think it's excellent:

> Holding onto unforgiveness is like drinking rat poison and expecting the rat to die.

I hope you caught the line from the Seventeenth-Century Nun's Prayer that said, "A sour [or bitter] old person is one of the crowning works of the Enemy." That's why the Bible warns us in Hebrews 12:15:

> See to it that no one misses the grace of God and that no bitter root grows up to cause trouble and defile many.
>
> Hebrews 12:15

I often tell people, if you won't let go of the bitterness for your own sake, do it for your children. They are the ones who suffer the most. They are the ones who are defiled. If you don't believe me, spend an hour with someone whose parents went through an acrimonious divorce. Such people usually have lots of free time because they are almost always single (they either never marry or can't seem to stay married). I want to hasten to add that it's not just divorced people who can become embittered. I happen to know the Queen of Porcupines, and she has been married to the same man for forty-five years.

I believe the key to forgiveness is asking God to help us see those who've hurt us through his eyes. A little com-

25

passion goes a long way when you're trying to put your problems into perspective. Everyone has a story to tell, and that's the truest sentence in this book. Yes, even the person who has hurt you most could write his or her very own Major Motion Picture script, and guess who the hero would be? Now here's a frightening thought: guess who the villain would be? YOU! Everyone who has ever hurt you has been hurt, too. And maybe that's why they hurt you.

> The key to forgiveness is asking God to help us see those who've hurt us through his eyes.

Significant people in your life have disappointed you . . . some in small ways, others profoundly so. You didn't sign up for disappointing relationships, but they signed up for you. Now the question remains: What will you do? Will you live your life consumed by the bitterness? Will you be a porcupine? Or will you allow God to heal the hurt?

Only you can decide.

I Think I May Be Dying

"I think there is something seriously wrong with me. I just know it. I found another lump yesterday."

So began a recent phone conversation with a certain woman who shall remain nameless. To be honest, she doesn't need a name because she could be almost any one of us, couldn't she? That is, any of us who dwell in Major Motion Pictureville. Have you ever noticed that certain women almost delight in discovering new signs and symptoms? They can take the most microscopic mole and turn it into the proverbial mountain. A woman once told me she was "deathly allergic" to chocolate and hadn't been able to have so much as a nibble of it in nearly a decade. *No chocolate EVER? How tragic*, I thought. *How could this dear saint endure?* Although I generally try to eat healthy (except when I'm on one of my famous binges), I couldn't fathom the misery of a life lived entirely devoid of the occasional Reese's Peanut Butter Cup.

I guess my life must be pretty dull because the thought of a chocolate-less existence haunted me for a number of weeks. I just couldn't shake the idea: *no chocolate? NO chocolate?* Wow. I knew the woman needed serious prayer support. Then I began to wonder exactly what she meant by "deathly allergic." If chocolate is enough to cause a near-death reaction in one woman, perhaps I had a civic responsibility to warn *all* women what might happen to them someday. The human body is always changing, and who knows? Someday, you might wake up to discover *you* have contracted this deadly allergy.

So I finally asked her, with a tinge of fear in my voice, "What exactly happens to you when you eat chocolate?"

To which she replied with great conviction, "Oh, my skin breaks out terribly."

There you have it. A near-death experience. I can read the obituary now:

> DEATH BY CHOCOLATE
> April 29, 2004. Anywhere, USA. Unsweetened church lady dies of three large pimples after eating a Kit Kat bar. Closed casket ceremony to be held at the First Christian Church.

I had another friend who was allergic to every food item on the planet except tofu. She was certain her kids had various food allergies too, because they would get "incredibly hyper" each day, then "crash" in the afternoon. It never occurred to her that their "incredibly hyper" behavior was simply called playing and the dramatic "crash" was called a nap. Children have been playing and taking naps since the dawn of time. But not at her house. At her house, it was a dramatic production, a Major Motion Picture requiring advanced medical testing and constant vigilance on her part.

That's not to say you shouldn't keep tabs on your body so you can alert your doctor if you see or feel anything unusual. Nor am I saying there's no such thing as food allergies or that you shouldn't safeguard your children's health. I'm talking about *keeping things in perspective.*

I'll be the first to admit that there have been many, many times in my life when I was absolutely certain I had contracted a dread disease. For some reason, I usually suspected leukemia. Even though I have no clue what the actual symptoms of the disease are, that didn't prevent me from diagnosing myself with it on numerous occasions. My first thought, right after "I think I'm dying," was almost always "I'm going to write a book about it, then they'll make it into a movie and the whole world will know how much I suffered." No doubt about it. Few things, other than a dreadful childhood or a natural disaster, make for a Major Motion Picture quite like a serious illness. From *Love Story* to *Terms of Endearment* and *A Walk to Remember*, the world is captivated by the tale of a dying person. That's why I almost *savored* the thought that there was something seriously wrong with me: *Now they'll be sorry for the way they treated me! Now they'll realize what a gem of a person I am. Now they'll finally see the truth! Everyone who's ever kicked me around will be forced to admit, before I take my last breath, that they were all wrong.*

Alas, it always turned out that my only problems were eating too many refined carbohydrates and emotionally exhausting myself by transforming my most minor setback into a Major Motion Picture.

One of the saddest stories I know involves a woman who has spent her entire life dying. In fact, she's been so busy convincing herself—and trying to convince everyone around her—that she's dying, that she has forgotten to live. She's now in her eighties, and despite her dread diseases both real and imagined, she's managed to live as long as or longer than most people on the planet ever will. But rather than living all those years, she's been dying all those years.

A friend of mine who works as a nurse in the rural South told me an absolutely hilarious true story about another woman who was a bundle of ailments. She came to the clinic every week complaining of some sickness or another. One week, she achieved the ultimate: her very own near-death experience. Traveling home from the clinic, she had to drive beneath a newly constructed underpass. As she did, she heard a loud popping sound and felt something hit the back of her head. She reached back and felt a gooey ooze. She rushed to the nearest Emergency Room and ran in screaming, "I've been shot! I've been shot!" The doctors examined her and discovered Pillsbury dinner rolls on the back of her head—a can had exploded in the backseat of her car.

Only a true Drama Queen can convince herself that she's been *shot by a sniper on the overpass*, when in point of fact she has tonight's dinner rolls stuck to the back of her head.

What a pathetic commentary on the loneliness of our culture that some people feel the only way they can get any love or attention is to get sick. Hypochondria is defined as "a mental disorder characterized by a preoccupation with bodily functions and the interpretation of normal sensations or minor abnormalities as indications of highly disturbing problems needing medical attention." Interestingly enough, a further symptom of hypochondria is that hypochondriacs have no clue that they are actually suffering from Major Motion Picture-itis. In fact, rather than being reassured when the doctor tells them they're making a mountain out of a lump of cellulite, "Negative results of diagnostic evaluations and reassurance by physicians only *increase* the patient's anxious concern about his health and the patient continues to seek medical attention."[1] Talk about your vicious cycles. Yikes!

Of course, I'm certain none of you are hypochondriacs, so let's move on to the problem many of us actually have: literally being sick, as opposed to merely imagining that we are sick.

Temples or Trash Cans?

I'm so glad I'm not a doctor. Not that I need to be, because all I have to do is go to a church prayer meeting and I get an earful of medical reports. I'm continually amazed at the number of women, yes, even Christian women, who seem to think their physical ailments constitute a fascinating topic of conversation. Not that I'm casting the first stone, because I used to be the worst offender! I spent the better part of two decades chronically ill, so I know what it feels like to be sick

> Hypochondriacs have no clue that they are actually suffering from Major Motion Picture-itis.

and tired of feeling sick and tired. If it wasn't one thing, it was another. Sinus headaches, allergies, migraines, strep throat, upper respiratory infections, stomach viruses, not to mention every cold and flu that came down the pike. I was constantly on antibiotics, sulfur drugs, decongestants, and allergy medications. I had a bottle of prescription cough medicine with codeine on hand at all times. It was like my American Express card. I did not leave home without it. I think I was single-handedly keeping the pharmaceutical companies in business. You know what's sad? During all those years, I was a Christian. I loved God, but I was still a physical wreck. Sick and tired. Sick and tired. That was my life. You know what, sisters? Praise God. I can honestly say I don't live like that anymore. I truly don't. Not that I have been transformed into Barbie with a Bible and all my problems have disappeared. I still have "those days," but it's not who I am. I am not chronically sick anymore . . . and I was *for years*. I am not chronically depressed . . . and I was *for years*.

The Bible has real answers for the mess we're in. Not magic formulas. This is real life, not a Major Motion Picture. The Bible isn't a magic wand we can wave over our problems, but I have found within its pages a pathway to health and wholeness. It's changed my life, and I want to share it with you.

Are you sick and tired of feeling sick and tired? The problem is rampant in the church. A Christian magazine conducted a nationwide survey of pastors and discovered that 80 percent of all church prayer requests are related to health concerns. In my previous book *This Isn't the Life I Signed Up For*, I explored a variety of causes for sickness and disease. It's not my intention to revisit that subject here, except to say as clearly as I can: most of us are *making ourselves sick*, or at the very least, we're not doing enough to keep ourselves healthy.

An increasing body of medical science provides compelling proof that 70 percent of degenerative diseases are directly related to our lifestyles.[2] Too many of us Christian women treat our bodies, which are the temples of the Holy Spirit, like trash cans by filling ourselves with junk food, soda, and coffee. Once upon a time, gluttony was considered one of the Seven Deadly Sins. The church took overeating very seriously. Now it's commonplace. Have you ever heard a sermon preached against overeating? I think it's interesting that the fall of mankind involved a woman being tempted by food that looked too good to pass up:

> When the woman saw that the fruit of the tree was good for food and pleasing to the eye, and also desirable for gaining wisdom, she took some and ate it. She also gave some to her husband, who was with her, and he ate it. Then the eyes of both of them were opened, and they realized they were naked; so they sewed fig leaves together and made coverings for themselves.
>
> Genesis 3:6–7

Notice how, after Eve demonstrated her inability to practice self-control in the presence of tempting food, the first thing she needed was a new outfit. Sound familiar? I don't know about you, but I am certainly in no position to judge Eve. I love food that looks good to eat: donuts, cookies, cakes. I often engage in what I call "punishment eating." When someone hurts my feelings, I punish them by downing a gallon of ice cream. I'm as guilty as the next woman of indulging my taste buds from time to time, even though I know these foods will lead me into sin. How? By altering my blood sugar and making me irritable within thirty minutes.

It's interesting that the fall of mankind involved a woman being tempted by food that looked too good to pass up.

Then I get depressed because my clothes don't fit. Like most women, I have three sizes in my closet: the size I *should* wear, the size I *usually* wear, and the size I'm

33

wearing when my kids know to run for the hills when I wake up in the morning. (At our house, an overweight mommy is a Grumpy Mommy.)

Is it just me or does eating all that junk literally make you feel sick? And if you go on a two-week binge, do you sometimes feel like you're dying? Yeah. Me, too.

I'm not saying we should all starve ourselves so we can look like movie stars performing on the screen of our very own Major Motion Picture. I'm saying we need to use wisdom when dealing with food issues. In addition to overeating—and all the problems it creates—many people are stumbling into bulimia, anorexia, and other eating disorders. Ask the Holy Spirit to lead you into a balanced approach to your eating habits.

> Since we have these promises, dear friends, let us purify ourselves from everything that contaminates body and spirit, perfecting holiness out of reverence for God.
>
> 2 Corinthians 7:1

Ask yourself, are the foods I'm eating purifying—or contaminating—my body? It's important to find a healthy balance between caring too much and too little about your body. Some women obsess over their personal appearance and go into emotional meltdown if they are fifteen pounds overweight. (I should know since I'm one of them.) Other women completely neglect their appearance, saying such concerns are unspiritual. Of course, this argument would hold weight (pun intended) if these women devoted all of their time to spiritual pursuits rather than exercising for thirty minutes per day. But we all know that's not the case. It's just an excuse.

If you are too busy to exercise thirty minutes a day, you are busier than God wants you to be. My guess is that you are telling yourself how indispensable you are to everyone at every moment of the day. Reality check: the world will continue revolving if you set aside thirty minutes to go take a walk. The house won't fall apart while you're gone; your husband and kids will do just fine without you. In fact, a little absence might make their hearts grow fonder. Better still, take your family with you on the walk.

Many women don't exercise at all because they think they have to undertake some grand exercise regime. If they can't spend two hours at the gym in a valiant, life-and-death battle to transform themselves into a size 8 within twelve weeks, then it's not worth the effort. Wrong! Your exercise program doesn't have to constitute an Oscar-winning performance. It doesn't have to be a competition. You don't have to enter a marathon. There's no need to imagine yourself the female version of Rocky (although I must admit I enjoy playing the Rocky sound track while I bounce on my mini-trampoline). It doesn't have to be a big production. Just put on a pair of sneakers and take a walk around the block.

> Your body is a tool to serve God. It's the only living sacrifice you have to offer him.

Your body is a tool to serve God. It's the only living sacrifice you have to offer him. Don't let your body turn into a tyrant, determining what you can and cannot do. You're supposed to be in charge, so take charge! The next time your body tells you, "I'm tired. Let's lie on the couch eating potato chips," say, "No, body. You are not in charge. I am the brains in this operation. And I say we are going to get up, grab a bottle of water, and take a walk. While we're at it, we're going to recite some Scripture memory verses. Then we're going to pray for our neighbors. So there, body, take that."

Give Me a Major Motion Picture Miracle!

Another way Major Motion Picture mode can manifest in the area of sickness is in our desire for a dramatic healing. Doesn't everyone want to experience a miracle? Wouldn't that be awesome? Not only to feel the power of God at work in your life, but then to stand up at church and tell everyone what God has done in your life? Wow! Sign me up! I'll take the starring role in that one!

Over the course of the last few months, I have witnessed a miracle up close and personal. Aly Pflugfedder, a thirty-two-year-old mother of three, attended the weekly Bible study I teach at my home church. In January 2004, she was diagnosed with possible ovarian cancer, a tumor on her pituitary gland, and cysts on her thyroid. We began a forty-day fast to pray for her healing. On March 3, 2004, the surgeons opened her up, and much to their surprise, found no malignancies despite every test indicating she was riddled with cancer. She had a hysterectomy since she was prone to ovarian cancer, but her body has been restored back to normal health faster than anyone could have anticipated. Aly says she wants to shout from the mountaintops what God has done in her life. She truly is a living testimony to the power of God and has experienced a miracle worthy of a Major Motion Picture.

But I believe we often overlook the ordinary miracles God performs in our everyday lives, just because they are *not* dramatic or Major Motion Picture–sized. Let me introduce you to someone who was determined to settle for nothing less than an Oscar-worthy miracle:

Now Naaman was commander of the army of the king of Aram. He was a great man in the sight of his master and highly regarded, because through him the LORD had given victory to Aram. He was a valiant soldier, but he had leprosy.

Now bands from Aram had gone out and had taken captive a young girl from Israel, and she served Naaman's wife. She said to her mistress, "If only my master would see the prophet who is in Samaria! He would cure him of his leprosy."

Naaman went to his master and told him what the girl from Israel had said. "By all means, go," the king of Aram replied. "I will send a letter to the king of Israel." So Naaman left, taking with him ten talents of silver, six thousand shekels of gold and ten sets of clothing. The letter that he took to the king of Israel read: "With this letter I am sending my servant Naaman to you so that you may cure him of his leprosy."

As soon as the king of Israel read the letter, he tore his robes and said, "Am I God? Can I kill and bring back to life? Why does this fellow send someone to me to be cured of his leprosy? See how he is trying to pick a quarrel with me!"

When Elisha the man of God heard that the king of Israel had torn his robes, he sent him this message: "Why have you torn your robes? Have the man come to me and he will know that there is a prophet in Israel." So Naaman went with his horses and chariots and stopped at the door of Elisha's house. Elisha sent a messenger to say to him, "Go, wash yourself seven times in the Jordan, and your flesh will be restored and you will be cleansed."

But Naaman went away angry and said, "I thought that he would surely come out to me and stand and call on the name of the LORD his God, wave his hand over the spot and cure me of my leprosy. Are not Abana and Pharpar, the rivers of Damascus, better than any of the waters of Israel? Couldn't I wash in them and be cleansed?" So he turned and went off in a rage.

2 Kings 5:1–12

Why was Naaman so furious? Because no doubt he had formulated in his own mind exactly how the miracle would take place: Drama. That's what he was hoping for. Maybe Elisha would have dozens of people dancing and chanting in a circle around him, as others pounded their drums. Surely, a large audience of locals would gather to witness this auspicious occasion, then honor him in a special ceremony acknowledging how he had been handpicked by God to be the beneficiary of such a powerful miraculous encounter.

Elisha didn't even come out of the house to see Naaman! What an insult. Instead, he sent out an underling with instructions for Naaman to go wash in the Jordan River seven times. He might just as well have told him to "go jump in a lake." That's why Naaman blew a gasket. He was insulted that Elisha wasn't making a big deal out of his healing. Where was the excitement? Where was the melodrama? How can you make a Major Motion Picture about someone dunking himself in a river?

The church today is filled with people who are afflicted in spirit, soul, and body, and many are seeking miraculous cures. And yes, I believe God still performs miracles today. But far more often, God simply says, as Elisha said to Naaman, "Wash and be cleansed." For most of us, healing is not found in the extraordinary but in the ordinary—simple things we take for granted; simple things we often neglect.

Yes, God can heal the sick through miraculous intervention, but isn't it a miracle that he created human beings with the ability to find cures for so many diseases? And isn't it an even greater miracle that our bodies were created to heal themselves? Cuts, bruises, sore throats, and headaches all remind us that, even without human intervention, our bodies can often heal. Isn't it a miracle that God placed healing foods (enriched with vitamins, minerals, and vital nutrients) on the earth: fruits, vegetables, herbs, and grains? Isn't it a miracle that these foods have the power to fortify against disease? Isn't it a miracle that we can alter our bodies just by altering the foods we eat?

Yes, God can bring emotional healing in a dramatic way through a powerful prayer warrior interceding on our behalf, but far more healing is brought about in human hearts through daily meditation on God's Word.

Yes, God can appoint someone to "speak a word" into your life, but is it any less miraculous that he has preserved his Word through thousands of years of war and disaster? Think of the tyrants through the ages who have tried to destroy the Bible, yet it has endured. What a miracle!

And isn't it miraculous that we have the ability to read? That our eyes can look at markings on a page, and somehow, those markings can change who we are and how we live?

Let's not overlook the ordinary miracles that surround us every day. Do you need a miracle in your life? If God were to tell you, right now, to do some dramatic thing, my guess is that you would probably do it. But maybe God is urging you to avail yourself of the ordinary miracles he has already provided. Several years ago on New Year's Eve, our pastor urged us to bow our heads and ask God for a mighty miracle in the coming year. Do you know what God spoke to my heart that late December evening? He said, "Donna, if you really want to see a mighty miracle in your life, learn to do smaller things with greater faithfulness."

Smaller things with greater faithfulness. That's where the real power in the Christian life comes from. Before we ask for divine intervention and mighty miracles, let's be faithful to avail ourselves of the power of the ordinary miracles he has already provided.

Then, rather than sitting around thinking *I may be dying*, you can stand up and shout, "Thank God, I'm finally LIVING!"

My Poor Nerves

"You have no idea how I suffer with my poor nerves," declares the high-strung mother in *Pride and Prejudice*. To which her husband calmly responds, "You are wrong, my dear. I have a high regard for your poor nerves. They have been my constant companion these twenty-nine years." Something tells me husbands around the world might declare a hearty Amen to that one. Women and their poor nerves! Today, we call it mood swings, PMS, depression, or the Change. Call it what you want, women have long allowed their emotions to rule their lives. The results are always destructive. In the last chapter, we looked at some of the reasons why we sometimes feel like we "may be dying," among them treating our bodies like trash cans. But you know what's even worse? What's really messing up our lives, our health, and our relationships? We're a bunch of nervous wrecks!

Since I've pretty much been an emotional basket case for the past month (as I've struggled to finish this book), I can definitely give a witness on this topic! Just the other day my husband said, "The problem is that when *you're* stressed out, it affects everybody around you." As the old saying goes, "If mamma ain't happy, ain't nobody happy." And lots of mammas ain't happy these days. Their misery is literally making them and the people around them sick. (Just as an aside, have you ever uttered the words, "You make me sick"? I'm sure you haven't, but has anyone ever said them to you? Sad to say, this expression can actually be true. Humans can literally affect one another's health.)

Someday I'm going to write a book about a subject I *have* mastered. But, to borrow a phrase from Aragorn in *The Return of the King*, "It is not this day." Today I write from the battlefront on a subject where the war still rages and I've yet to secure the victory. Truth be told, I was handed a mighty defeat just last night. So this morning, I don't feel like an "expert" on the Christian life or anything else. I don't feel qualified to impart to you my "superior wisdom and insight." Part of me wants to put down the pen and close up the laptop. Maybe wait until I've got the answers and then start writing. Instead, I'm pressing on. I made a decision long ago that my job was simply to share my life journey with anyone who wanted to walk a mile or two in my company.

I just wanted you to know that what I'm about to cover are the things God is still trying to get through my thick skull. Alas, I seem determined to keep going around the same dumb mountain, while God is equally determined for me to go round and round until I finally learn my lesson. Someday I'm going to ace one of these tests. Someday, but it is not this day. This day, I fight. Meanwhile, the answers are all in God's Word, and truth is true whether or not I choose to walk in the light of it. With those provisos in mind, here we go.

If there's one area that has caused me enough grief to constitute a Major Motion Picture, it's my haywire emotions. When we follow our feelings rather than walking in obedience, we are on a path guaranteeing one mishap after another.

The first hymn I remember singing as a new believer was "Trust and Obey."

> Trust and obey, for there's no other way
> To be happy in Jesus, but to trust and obey.

If I had taken those words to heart, the last twenty-four years would have been a completely different experience. I'd have a lot more friends and a lot fewer regrets. Something tells me I'm not alone, because I meet a lot of hurting Christian women. Somehow, we think we can doubt and disobey, but still be happy. It doesn't work. We've got to trust God and do what he says.

> Doubt and disobey, for there's no other way
> To be miserable as a Christian, but to doubt and
> disobey.

I know what you're thinking: *Doubt and disobey? Well, thankfully I don't do either of those things.* How do I know that's what you're thinking? Because that's exactly what *I* was thinking when God sat me down and said, "We need to talk." That was about five years ago. At the time, I was very busy doing two things: (1) congratulating myself for not being a "sinner" anymore, and (2) trying to figure out why my life was such a mess. I'd been a Christian for nearly twenty years and had shared my mess-timony—oops, I mean testimony—with people all over the world. It was such a blessing to be able to tell how God had delivered me instantly from drugs. He'd brought me out of my bondage to blatant sin, out of the land of Egypt. Naturally, I was not quite so eager to mention that I hadn't exactly marched directly to the Promised Land. In fact, I was still wandering around in the wilderness. Frankly, on some days, I still am. I apparently have dual citizenship in the Desert of Testing and the Promised Land, so I can journey back and forth at will.

You see, I wasn't a drug addict anymore. That's the good news. Someone could definitely make a triumphant Major Motion Picture about that part. Now for the bad part: I was a lonely and confused middle-aged woman, fast becoming a lonely and confused *old* woman long before my time. I was a Christian, and I did all the right things. I went to church instead of the bar. I read my Bible instead of trashy novels. I watched Veggie Tales instead of R-rated movies. I wrote to my congressman whenever he failed to defend family values. I even home-schooled my kids in a valiant attempt to raise up the next generation of mighty warriors for Jesus. I was doing everything I knew how to do to make the Christian life work.

> I apparently have dual citizenship in the Desert of Testing and the Promised Land, so I can journey back and forth at will.

But it wasn't working. As I've previously admitted, I was a physical and emotional wreck, but I couldn't figure out why. Bad genes? Dumb luck? Maybe the devil was attacking me or the world was out to get me. Then I reached that beautiful place called rock bottom and was ready to admit just how powerless I was in the face of the out-of-control emotions that governed my life.

So I picked up my prayer journal and I wrote down a question for God that became a turning point in my life. Before I go any further, let me stop and say that writing out a question for God is an incredibly powerful spiritual exercise. I would urge you to try it. Just get out a blank notebook and write out, in question form, whatever is bothering you. Then watch for the answer. That's the whole key. I believe God is constantly speaking into our lives, but since we aren't expecting him to say anything, we don't realize what's happening. It's like you're standing in a crowded room and someone looks at you and starts answering a question you didn't ask. The first words out of your mouth would probably be, "Are you talking to me?"

So write it down and pay attention to what happens next. Then you won't have to wonder if God is talking to you. You'll have your answer. Here's the burning question I asked:

What is the source and the solution to my chronic illness?

About a week later, God gave me a clear and compelling answer on the pages of a devotional book entitled *Come Away, My Beloved,* by Frances Roberts:

> How can I give you healing for your body while there is anxiety in your mind? So long as there is dis-ease in your thoughts, there shall be disease in your body. You have need of many things, but one thing in particular you must develop for your own preservation, and that is an absolute confidence in my loving care.
>
> "Come unto Me," it is written, "all ye that labor and are heavy-laden, and I will give you rest" (Matt. 11:28). Only when your mind is at rest can your body build health. Worry is an actively destructive force. Anxiety produces tension, and tension is the road to pain. Fear is devastating to the physical well-being of the body.

Anger throws poison into the system that no anti-biotic ever can counteract.

Ten minutes of unbridled temper can waste enough strength to do a half-day of wholesome work. Your physical energy is a gift from God, entrusted to you to be employed for His glory. It is a sin to take His gift and dissipate it through the trap doors of the evil emotions of the disposition.

Look not upon others and condemn them for jeopardizing their health by harmful habits [smoking, drinking, drugs, illicit sex] and wasting energies on vain pursuits while you yourself undermine your health by unworthy emotions, and take time, which by keeping your mind in an attitude of praise and faith, could be constructively employed, but instead you allow this time to be a period of destructive action by entertaining such things as self-pity and remorse and evil-surmisings.[1]

That was my answer. And although I still have a long way to go in terms of implementing that answer, at least I'm not wandering around in the dark anymore. At least there's a cloud of smoke by day and pillar of fire by night. At least I know I'm heading in the right direction, and that's got to be worth something. I want to take a quick look at what the Bible says about each of these emotions that can wreak havoc on our poor nerves, not to mention on our poor friends and relatives. Before I do, I want to ask you a simple question: When God tells you to do something and you do the opposite, what is that called? It's called sin. Even if it isn't immoral or illegal. Even if it doesn't appear to

> Emotions can wreak havoc on our poor nerves, not to mention on our poor friends and relatives.

be a blatant attack on the moral fiber of our nation, if God says Don't and you Do, that's a sin. It's called disobedience. Remember my little ditty about Doubt and Disobey? When you finish this chapter, you may change your mind about whether or not it applies to your life.

1. Worry

The first church-sanctioned sin we need to explore is worry. Ironically, not only can you get away with this one, but people will actually applaud you for being such a "concerned" person. We even have "concerned" citizens and "concerned" leaders. But Jesus said,

> Who of you by worrying can add a single hour to his life?
>
> Matthew 6:27

Worry is nothing more than glorified doubt. When you worry about clothes or food or what might happen tomorrow; when you worry about your kids and your husband's job; when you worry about how many people will attend the church-sponsored event you are planning, you are doubting God. And yes, when you worry that America is going down the tubes, you are doubting the God who said,

> If my people, who are called by my name, will humble themselves and pray and seek my face . . . I will hear from heaven . . . and will heal their land.
>
> 2 Chronicles 7:14

By focusing your mental energies on things that God could easily take care of if you simply asked him, you are

47

saying, "I doubt God. I don't think he is really looking out for me. I have to look out for myself. I can't trust God to watch out for my family and finances (or this nation, for that matter), so I'll have to handle it instead."

People claim they just can't memorize Scripture. It's too hard or they don't have the time. But all you have to do to memorize Scripture is meditate on it frequently. What is worry? Worry is nothing more than meditation because meditation is just thinking about the same thing over and over and over. Isn't it interesting that the same woman who can't memorize a single Bible verse can recite chapter and verse on all of her problems and her husband's faults? It's no mystery. God is a genius, and when he created the human brain—including your brain—he fashioned a masterpiece that absolutely, positively will remember whatever you play over and over in your head.

Then God gives you the choice. What do you want to remember? His goodness and mercy? Or the time your former best friend hurt your feelings? Whatever you think about over and over will seep down into your soul and become the very fabric of your being. The problem is, you are meditating on your problems. What possible good can that do you? So take the same skill you have developed through years of worrying—that is, the ability to play the same record over and over again—and put it to good use.

The expression "worried sick" should give us pause to consider whether worry is the best investment of our time! In contrast, the Bible says meditating on God's Word can literally bring physical and emotional healing:

> My son, pay attention to what I say;
> listen closely to my words.
> Do not let them out of your sight,
> keep them within your heart;

48

for they are life to those who find them
and health to a man's whole body.

Proverbs 4:20–22

Let me give you a practical tip for how you can work this out in your own life. If you have a prescription medication you take every day, write this on a label and affix it to the bottle: *Take medication with meditation.*

I don't take prescription medication anymore (you have no idea what a triumph that is). However, I do take nutritional supplements (visit www.donnapartow.com for my recommendations). I keep them in a basket on my kitchen counter. In the basket, I have placed a bunch of Scripture verse cards. Each morning, as I drink my protein shake and take my supplements, I review a few verses. It's that simple. I often tell women that if they will add a little meditation to their medication, they may find that eventually they will need less medication. Sure enough, I've had numerous women take me up on the challenge and email me later to say, "I went back to my doctor, and he decided to lower my blood pressure medication."

Jesus said, "Do not worry" (Matt. 6:25). That wasn't a suggestion; it was a command. The cure for worry is meditation.

2. Anxiety

If worry is all about "What if such and such doesn't happen?" anxiety goes a step beyond to ask, "What if it does?" How many of us lie awake at night, wracked with anxiety, imagining twists and turns that would make a Major Motion Picture look dull? What if this, what if that, what if the other thing? You think that doesn't

49

take a toll on your health and your poor nerves? Think again.

> Rejoice in the Lord always. I will say it again: Rejoice! Let your gentleness be evident to all. The Lord is near. Do not be anxious about anything, but in everything, by prayer and petition, with thanksgiving, present your requests to God. And the peace of God, which transcends all understanding, will guard your hearts and your minds in Christ Jesus.
>
> Finally, brothers, whatever is true, whatever is noble, whatever is right, whatever is pure, whatever is lovely, whatever is admirable—if anything is excellent or praiseworthy—think about such things. Whatever you have learned or received or heard from me, or seen in me—put it into practice. And the God of peace will be with you.
>
> Philippians 4:4–9

What is the cure for anxiety? Prayer. It's a cliché but it works: you may not know what the future holds, but if you know who holds the future, what are you freaking out about? We're back to doubt and disobey, aren't we? You don't really believe God when he says "The Lord is near," and you choose to disobey him when he says, "Do not be anxious" but instead "pray." However, if you will choose to trust and obey, God will give you the peace that transcends all understanding. That, of course, is the real problem for us. We don't want the peace that doesn't make sense—a peace despite our circumstances. We want the peace that makes perfect sense because our circumstances are peaceful and life always goes our way. But God doesn't promise us that kind of peace. The Hebrew word for peace is *shalom*, which means wholeness or total well-being in your spirit, soul, and body. That's what God wants for his children. He wants us to be able to say, no matter what happens, "It is well with my soul." Because a peace that depends on peaceful circumstances is not worth having.

3. Fear

No doubt you've heard the expression that 90 percent of what we fear never happens. What a waste of time and emotional energy. Fear is truly a destructive emotion because it releases a chemical called adrenaline into the bloodstream. You've heard the phrase "scared to death." It can literally be true. Too much adrenaline can bring on a heart attack. Even a lifetime of low-level fear can wipe out your adrenal glands, which is particularly debilitating to women and can lead to osteoporosis and various complications during menopause—and yes, to premature death. God cares about our poor nerves because, among other things, he doesn't want our lives cut short. That's why the Bible commands us, eighty-three times, "Do not fear." Can you guess what the opposite of fear is? Trust. The word *trust* occurs eighty-seven times. Here's a good example:

Fear not, for I have redeemed you;
    I have summoned you by name; you are mine.
When you pass through the waters,
    I will be with you;
and when you pass through the rivers,
    they will not sweep over you.
When you walk through the fire,
    you will not be burned; . . .
For I am the LORD, your God,
    the Holy One of Israel, your Savior; . . .
Since you are precious and honored in my sight,
    and because I love you,

51

I will give men in exchange for you,
    and people in exchange for your life.
Do not be afraid, for I am with you.

Isaiah 43:1–5

Notice that God doesn't say, "Nothing scary will ever happen to you. I'm going to set your life up so that you have nothing to fear." Quite the opposite. The clear implication from this passage is that you are going to encounter situations where the most natural thing in the world is to be "scared to death." Raging rivers, burning fires. Any woman in her right mind would be afraid of such things. We could easily add to the list teenagers and menopause, because those are equally frightening. But God is saying, "I want you to look fearful situations in the eye and make a conscious decision to trust me anyway. I want you to trust me, knowing that I love you and will take care of you." The cure for fear is trust.

4. Anger

Of all the people I know who honest-to-goodness could qualify for a Lifetime Movie Special, my friend Rachel would be at the top. She married a superrich, handsome, charming guy who turned out to be a wife-beating alcoholic at home, even while continuing to run a multimillion-dollar enterprise. When Rachel's husband died of an overdose at the age of thirty-seven, his mother blamed Rachel, which was ridiculous because Rachel was powerless to stop her husband's addiction. And few people suffered more because of him than Rachel and her three small children. Nevertheless, her mother-in-law hired attorneys to literally rob Rachel and her children of the inheritance that was due to them. She did everything in her power to make their lives more difficult. Almost every time I talked to Rachel, she would be angry and upset about the situation. Justifiably so, I might add.

One day, as she was getting worked up about the latest rotten thing her mother-in-law had done, I said: "She sounds like she's in a lot of pain. She doesn't want to face the truth about her son. I think you should pray for her." She later told me that praying really changed her heart toward her mother-in-law, even though it didn't change her mother-in-law's behavior. The woman is now dying, so Rachel took the children to visit her. They were able to speak kindly to their grandmother, viewing her through their mother's eyes of compassion. Most important, Rachel felt wonderful because she did not let this angry person turn her into an angry person.

Believe it or not, the cure for anger is compassion. It's learning to see the person who hurt you as a hurting person. Think about someone you are angry at right now. Rather than recounting your melodrama to everyone around you, stop and pray. Ask God to help you see that person through his eyes of compassion. I once heard it said that you will know you have forgiven someone when something good happens to that person and you are genuinely happy. I remember thinking, *Yeah, right. Clearly you don't know what that person did to me!* However, I began to pray, asking God for his compassion. About a month ago, the person I used to be so angry with did indeed have something wonderful happen. And I was honestly happy. The mere fact that I was happy made me even happier, because I saw that there was hope for "my poor nerves" after all. We don't have to be ruled by our feelings; we can learn to live differently. Our Major Motion Picture can have a happy ending, if we will obey God when he tells us, "Do not let the sun go down while you are still angry, and do not give the devil a foothold" (Eph. 4:26–27).

5. Self-Pity

I must admit that this is the toughest one for me to address, because I still struggle with this big-time. Even though this book's title is meant to be humorous, I truly have lived most of my life as if everything that happened to me was dreadful enough to warrant a Major Motion Picture. And if things didn't seem quite large enough to start with, I developed the gift of blowing things out of proportion. Fortunately, I'm not as bad as I used to be, and I find some consolation in that.

The truth is, I was literally consumed with self-pity, and it almost destroyed me. Poor, poor pitiful me. How the world had done me wrong! How I met with injustice and ill-treatment at every turn! No one could get within a mile of me without hearing a litany of my woes. Yet I couldn't figure out why my phone never rang. Could there be a connection? I didn't think so either.

I had one person in particular I liked to complain to, because she not only listened sympathetically, but she would add a little commentary that confirmed she knew the magnitude of my suffering. I'll call her Cindy. I figured it was good for Cindy to listen to my woes, since she drove a nice car and her husband had a great job. Besides, she always had a great big smile on her face and obviously had life made in the shade. At least, she never indicated having any problems of her own. So I was performing an important public service by helping her keep in touch with the lives of poor, disadvantaged people such as myself, those who "suffer the slings and arrows of outrageous fortune."

Then one day a mutual friend mentioned in passing that Cindy was dying. "Dying? As in *dying* dying? But she's only in her forties. How is that possible?" I asked in amazement. It turns out that Cindy had contracted an incurable disease several years earlier and had been battling it ever since. She had been through several rounds of chemotherapy; but there was no cure. Cindy was dying. But Cindy was remarkably happy. And do you know why? Because Cindy refused to wallow in self-pity, and she didn't waste her time trying to solicit other people's pity, either. That's why she never once mentioned her terminal illness to me, in between my pitiful tales of burnt toast and fat thighs—although she did share this sage advice with me one day: "You know, Donna, everybody has their own bag of rocks to carry."

And I started to think about that. Everyone has their own bag of rocks. Everyone has their own war stories. Their own heartaches. What right do I have to ask other people to carry my bag in addition to their own? What right did I have to burden down this dying woman with my never-ending self-pity trip?

No right at all. That's why Jesus told us to lay our burdens down at his feet, to make it easier for us to resist the temptation to lay them down at everyone else's door. Cast all your cares upon him, because he cares for you. He is the only one with the strength to carry your bag of rocks.

Depression sometimes has a biochemical basis. In particular, I think postpartum depression, PMS-related symptoms, and menopause are very real health challenges that may require medical attention and significant lifestyle changes. However, I also think a whole lot of depression is the natural outcome of wallowing in self-pity. You know, it is almost impossible to stay depressed without feeling sorry for yourself. If you're depressed, the best thing you can do is help someone else. If you're depressed because of a biochemical imbalance, reaching out won't hurt you, and it may just help by putting your problems into perspective. No matter how bad you think you've got it, there's always someone who is worse off. In fact, whenever I'm bored at my own little pity party, I watch *Out of Africa* or another movie about a woman who had real problems, but managed to rise above.

Thanks to Mel Gibson, we can now watch *The Passion of the Christ* and consider the suffering of Jesus, "who for the joy set before him endured the cross, scorning its shame, and sat down at the right hand of the throne of God" (Heb. 12:2). I don't know what you may be enduring in your life at this moment. It may be difficult, but it cannot compare with Golgotha, nor can it compare with what God has prepared for those who love him.

6. Remorse

In my ministry, I often talk about the damage done by our sinful response to the sin of others. However, remorse is our sinful response to our own sin. We actually need to repent of the sin of remorse. To repent means to "agree with God." Here's what God says:

> For as high as the heavens are above the earth,
>   so great is his love for those who fear him;
> as far as the east is from the west,
>   so far has he removed our transgressions from us.
>
> Psalm 103:11–12

If you keep rehearsing your past failures, drowning in a sea of regret, it's time to get into agreement with God and believe him when he says, "It's forgotten." There's no point dwelling on the past. You can't change it anyway. Even if you've made mistakes, all you can do is ask the forgiveness of those involved and perhaps make some form of restitution. Then you have to move forward, by throwing yourself at the foot of the cross and choosing to believe his grace is sufficient. When you beat yourself up, what you are actually saying is, "Those Roman soldiers didn't beat Jesus enough. I have to add a few lashes to his otherwise finished work." You are calling Jesus a liar, because he said, "It is finished," but you keep saying, "This isn't over yet." It's finished. It's over. Forgiven. Move on.

7. Evil-Surmisings

When I read *Come Away, My Beloved*, I wasn't quite sure what an evil-surmising was, so I did a little research! It means assuming the worst about people and situations or jumping to conclusions before you have all the information. I must be the Queen of Evil-Surmisings. If someone says, "I need to talk to you," my first thought is *She's mad at me. I've done something wrong.* I did this just recently. I had received several emails and a phone call about speaking for a major ministry conference. I was so excited, I was dancing for joy around my kitchen. No kidding! I sent a follow-up email confirming the details of our last conversation, and I didn't hear back for a week. Here come the evil-surmisings: they've changed their mind; they've rejected me; they've found out what a loser I am and decided to go with another speaker. I literally tormented myself. It turned out the woman was out of town.

Jacob was the King of Evil-Surmisings. Remember how he was so sure his brother Esau was going to kill him? Jacob was quick to believe Joseph had been torn apart by wild animals, even though it wasn't true.

Then they got Joseph's robe, slaughtered a goat and dipped the robe in the blood. They took the ornamented

57

robe back to their father and said, "We found this. Examine it to see whether it is your son's robe."

He recognized it and said, "It is my son's robe! Some ferocious animal has devoured him. Joseph has surely been torn to pieces."

Genesis 37:31–33

But he couldn't believe Joseph was second in command after Pharaoh, which *was* true:

So they went up out of Egypt and came to their father Jacob in the land of Canaan. They told him, "Joseph is still alive! In fact, he is ruler of all Egypt." Jacob was stunned; he did not believe them.

Genesis 45:25–26

Of course, the brothers were able to convince their father it was true, but only because of the overwhelming mountain of evidence they had brought back from Egypt. Weeks earlier, when God already had the wheels well in motion for his deliverance, Jacob had declared, "Everything is against me!" (Gen. 42:36). Even though Jacob loved God, he lived his whole life eager to believe the worst and slow to believe the best. Let's not be like that.

The mind is very complex, and it can play tricks on us. We can create problems out of thin air. Women are notorious for doing this to their husbands, especially when their husbands have to work late at night. Don't allow your mind to spiral out of control, imagining various scenarios and offenses. Discipline your mind to focus not on what "might" be true, but strictly on what you know to be true—for example: God's Word. Life is filled with enough troubles without manufacturing more in your head. Let your mind be filled with the things of the Spirit, which bring life and peace. I'm going to say a lot more about peace in the next chapter, but for now,

58

do yourself a favor and make a conscious decision to believe the best about people and situations until you have some solid evidence to the contrary.

"Love believes the best" according to 1 Corinthians 13. The Serenity Prayer sums it all up perfectly:

> God grant me the serenity to accept the things I cannot change,
> Courage to change the things I can,
> And the wisdom to know the difference.

If you want to give your "poor nerves" a rest, make a list of all the things you cannot change and choose to let them go. Don't waste your time and emotional energy on them:

- Your genetic makeup
- Your age—and the inevitable limitations of growing older and slowing down
- The reality of living in a fallen world with 6 billion sinful people who will inevitably let you down
- The very real fact that the devil is bad and he may attack you
- Your past: people who have hurt you and all the unfair stuff you've had to live through; the mistakes and foolish choices you've already made
- What might happen in the future
- Last but certainly not least: other people. You cannot change the choices they make or how they choose to treat you. You can't change what other people think, feel, and choose. You can get all upset when people say unfair or untrue things about you. Or you can trust God to handle the situation and believe that eventually the truth will prevail.

I often say, "Accept the things you cannot change or they will change you into someone you don't want to be!" But there's another part to the Serenity Prayer, and that's changing the things you can. Isn't it ironic how we waste countless hours every day focusing our energy on things we can't change, then complain that we don't have time to grow in our relationship with God? We don't have time to cultivate spiritual disciplines like prayer, studying the Bible, worship, or fellowship. We don't have time to exercise or eat right. Don't have time to nurture our family and friends. Yet somehow we manage to find time for worry, anxiety, fear, anger, self-pity, remorse, and evil-surmisings. We manage to find time for all of that nonsense.

I once attended a seminar on how to get more hours in my day. The truth is, we don't need more time. We just need to use the time we already have more productively. We need to take the same time and energy we squander on our "poor nerves" and channel it into creating positive change. We need to trade our worry for meditation, our anxiety for prayer, our fear for trust, our anger for compassion, our self-pity for outreach, our remorse for forgiveness, and our evil-surmisings for love. Then every moment we're awake will draw us closer to God and others.

> Accept the things you cannot change or they will change you into someone you don't want to be!

I want to go back to the excerpt from *Come Away, My Beloved*:

60

How can I give you healing for your body while there is anxiety in your mind? So long as there is dis-ease in your thoughts, there shall be disease in your body. You have need of many things, but one thing in particular you must develop for your own preservation, and that is an absolute confidence in my loving care.

That's the solution. That's the ultimate cure for all that ails our poor nerves, our aching bodies, and our strained relationships. "Absolute confidence in God's loving care." It's the health prescription I am now pursuing in my own life. It strikes me as perfectly logical that someone who doesn't trust God, who allows herself to worry and fret and fuss, will get sick a lot more often than someone whose mind is kept in perfect peace, focusing on the goodness of God and the loving care of our Jehovah Rapha, the Lord our healer, the Great Physician.

The best part about developing absolute confidence in God's loving care is that you can retain your confidence even in the very worst of circumstances. Horatio Spafford lost his only son to scarlet fever. Shortly thereafter, he suffered financial disaster in the Great Chicago Fire of 1871, which left three hundred people dead and a hundred thousand homeless. For the next two years, he worked tirelessly helping people rebuild their lives. In 1873, his friend Dwight L. Moody planned an evangelistic campaign in London. Spafford decided to help with the crusade, then take his remaining family members—his wife and four daughters—on a trip through Europe. At the last minute, Spafford had to stay in the U.S. on urgent business. The ship carrying his family on ahead was struck by another vessel and sank within twelve minutes. When his wife was brought ashore, she sent the now-famous cable to her husband, "Saved alone." All four of their daughters had drowned in the Atlantic Ocean.

Horatio Spafford booked passage on the next ship. As they were crossing the Atlantic Ocean, the captain called Spafford aside and pointed out the place where his daughters were likely to have drowned. He was certainly a prime candidate for worry, anxiety, fear, anger, self-pity, remorse, and evil-surmisings. Not to mention depression, suicide, and maybe even a heart attack on the spot. How many of us can even imagine facing such devastating losses?

Instead, Horatio Spafford's absolute confidence in God's loving care remained unshaken. That very night, he penned the words "When peace like a river attendeth my way, when sorrows like sea billows roll; whatever my lot, thou has taught me to say, it is well, it is well with my soul."

God wants to teach you to say, "It is well with my soul." And it will be, as you learn to trust and obey in all areas of your life. Yes, even when it comes to your poor nerves!

I Can't Seem to Get a Moment's Peace

Don't worry, God, I'll be running the world today. You can sit back and relax while I get things under control.

I sometimes wonder what God would do without all my help. I mean, I do so much: I keep track of everyone's schedule, I convict people of sin, I stay alert to hidden dangers, I nag my husband, I read my teenager's diary, I lie awake at night calculating and recalculating my debt ratios. Whew! I'm exhausted just thinking about it.

Good thing Jesus left me in charge.

What's that? He didn't leave me in charge? Oh, then what did he leave me?

> Peace I leave with you; my peace I give you. I do not give to you as the world gives. Do not let your hearts be troubled and do not be afraid.
>
> John 14:27

You're probably sitting there thinking, *Talk about your miscommunications! I had no clue! I thought I was doing God a big favor by carrying the weight of the world on my shoulders; now I come to find out all he wants me to do is chill out? Nobody tells me nothin'!*

Well, sister, I would have told you sooner if only I had known. But I just found out a short while ago. Hard to believe, especially by looking at the lifestyle of your average church lady, but apparently Jesus said he wants us to live in peace. In fact, the word *peace* occurs more than two hundred times in the Bible. Hopefully you recall from the last chapter that peace, or shalom, means wholeness and total well-being in spirit, soul, and body. Could you use a little of that?

In Mark 5:25–34, we encounter a woman who was obviously in desperate need of peace—wholeness in her spirit, soul, and body:

A large crowd followed and pressed around him. And a woman was there who had been subject to bleeding for twelve years. She had suffered a great deal under the care of many doctors and had spent all she had, yet instead of getting better she grew worse. When she heard about Jesus, she came up behind him in the crowd and touched his cloak, because she thought, "If I just touch his clothes, I will be healed." Immediately her bleeding stopped and she felt in her body that she was freed from her suffering.

At once Jesus realized that power had gone out from him. He turned around in the crowd and asked, "Who touched my clothes?"

"You see the people crowding against you," his disciples answered, "and yet you can ask, 'Who touched me?'"

But Jesus kept looking around to see who had done it. Then the woman, knowing what had happened to her, came and fell at his feet and, trembling with fear, told him the whole truth. He said to her, "Daughter, your faith has healed you. Go in peace and be freed from your suffering."

In chapter 2, we talked about hypochondriacs and women who either make themselves sick or don't do enough to keep themselves well. But now we encounter a woman with a serious health problem, who had obviously done everything she knew how to do to find healing. We know she needed physical healing, because she'd spent twelve long years being treated by physicians to no avail. But I think she also needed healing for her soul. This poor woman had spent all that time as a social outcast, because anyone with an issue of blood was declared unclean. She probably needed spiritual healing, as she had almost certainly been judged by the spiritual leaders of her day, who no doubt told her she was *to blame* and that there must be some sin in her life.

She was healed physically the moment she touched the hem of Jesus's garment, but that was *not enough* for Jesus. He wanted to do more than heal her physically; he wanted her to experience peace. Maybe Jesus knew that unless she was restored in spirit, soul, and body, she was very likely to become physically ill again. The Bible doesn't tell us the why, but it does tell us the what: he offered her peace. He offered her wholeness in spirit, soul, and body. He offers the same to you and me today.

I sometimes wonder what God would do without all my help.

One of the names of God is Jehovah Shalom or the Lord is Peace (Judges 6:24), and Jesus is called the Prince of Peace (Isa. 9:6). I have spent the last hour meditating on what God's Word says about how we find and cultivate peace in our lives and reap its rewards. It has been such a blessing to me. I'm literally sitting here with tears of joy in my eyes. I want you to experience the same blessing. So, even though I realize this is a departure from previous chapters, I want to give you an assignment. Slowly and prayerfully read through each passage that follows. Then, in the space provided, write what you learn about peace.

> I will lie down and sleep in peace, for you alone, O LORD, make me dwell in safety (Ps. 4:8).

_____

_____

_____

> The LORD gives strength to his people; the LORD blesses his people with peace (Ps. 29:11).

_____

_____

_____

> Seek peace and pursue it. The eyes of the LORD are on the righteous and his ears are attentive to their cry (Ps. 34:14–15).

_____

_____

_____

> I will listen to what God the LORD will say; he promises peace to his people, his saints—but let them not return to folly. Surely his salvation is near those who fear him, that his glory may dwell in our land. Love and faithfulness meet together; righteousness and peace kiss each other. Faithfulness springs forth from the earth, and righteousness looks down from heaven. The LORD will

indeed give what is good, and our land will yield its harvest (Ps. 85:8–12).

A heart at peace gives life to the body, but envy rots the bones (Prov. 14:30).

Better a dry crust with peace and quiet than a house full of feasting, with strife (Prov. 17:1).

You will keep in perfect peace him whose mind is steadfast, because he trusts in you (Isa. 26:3).

Lord, you establish peace for us; all that we have accomplished you have done for us (Isa. 26:12).

The fruit of righteousness will be peace; the effect of righteousness will be quietness and confidence forever (Isa. 32:17).

Those who walk uprightly enter into peace (Isa. 57:2).

Let us therefore make every effort to do what leads to peace and to mutual edification (Rom. 14:19).

May the God of hope fill you with all joy and peace as you trust in him, so that you may overflow with hope by the power of the Holy Spirit (Rom. 15:13).

Let the peace of Christ rule in your hearts (Col. 3:15).

First Thessalonians 5:23–24 captures the holistic nature of peace beautifully. Paul is writing a prayer for his fellow believers:

> May God himself, the God of peace, sanctify you through and through. May your whole spirit, soul and body be kept blameless at the coming of our Lord Jesus Christ. The one who calls you is faithful and he will do it.

I don't know about you, but I always thought the words *soul* and *spirit* were synonymous. Many people use them interchangeably, but this verse makes it plain that they are two different things. Your spirit is that part of your being where the Holy Spirit takes up residency; it is the portion that communes with God. Your soul, in contrast, encompasses your mind, your will, and your emotions. In other words, what you think, do, and feel. For many years, I was puzzled by the verse, "Work out your own salvation with fear and trembling" (Phil. 2:12 NKJV). I knew we couldn't earn our salvation, so what were we supposed to work on? Here's what I believe it means: take what God has already accomplished in your spirit and let it transform your soul—your mind, your will, and your emotions.

More than half of the New Testament books open with the phrase "Grace and Peace." Grace has to do with God's unmerited favor, by which he granted us entrance into the kingdom of God. It means that we will have the unspeakable joy of experiencing heaven in heaven. But peace is what we need here on earth. It's God's way of enabling us to experience a taste of heaven on earth.

But practically speaking, how do we enter into his peace? And why do so few Christians seem to experience it? From my observation, Christians tend to live at two extremes: those who drive themselves to physical and emotional exhaustion trying to please God, and those who are content to sneak into heaven by the skin of their teeth. Both approaches make excellent fodder for a Major Motion Picture, but the middle ground makes for sanity.

Let's take a look at both extremes and see if we can discover a place of peace somewhere in the middle. At one extreme you have legalism. Legalists can't get any rest because they are working so hard to make sure no one who wears the label "Christian" has any fun. Rather than Grace and Peace, they have Grace and Rules. Rules about what you can and cannot do, what you can wear and what you can watch, how to fix your hair—or how *not* to fix your hair, as the case may be.

69

Then they hunt through the Old Testament, picking and choosing which laws and rituals they want to abide by. So even though these Christians will enter heaven by God's grace, they certainly aren't experiencing a whole lot of peace on earth. And zilch on the goodwill toward men.

Have you ever noticed how these hardworking Christians seem mad all the time? It's quite remarkable! Just a few hours ago, I received an email from a total stranger who was absolutely furious with me. Apparently he heard the news that, after eighteen years as a battered wife and four years as a single mom, I had finally found a loving husband. (Actually my husband found me, but let's not quibble over minor details or I'll be tempted to shift into Major Motion Picture mode.) Well, this man wasn't about to sit idly by and wait for the Holy Spirit to convict me of the wickedness of my ways. No sir. God might be so preoccupied trying to rescue starving children in the Sudan or persecuted Christians in North Korea that he might not notice what's *really* wrong in the world today—like Donna Partow experiencing a little peace on earth. So, this man loaded up his Bible like a gun and fired off some verses to set me straight.

> Legalists can't get any rest because they are working so hard to make sure no one who wears the label "Christian" has any fun.

What an exhausting way to live! Can you imagine taking it on as your personal responsibility to email everyone on the planet who made a decision you disagreed with? *Yikes!* It reminds me of the woman who sent me a multiple-page letter instructing me on everything from which version of the Bible I should read to what church I should attend. Do these people ever sleep?

I prefer to live by the words of St. Augustine, "Love God and do whatever you want." Of course, people can take that to the other extreme. They are into Grace and Worldliness. Their attitude is, "Hey, I just pray the prayer and I'm good to go. I can do whatever I want 'cause I'm going to heaven anyway. I can watch R-rated movies. I can steal office supplies from my employer. I can cheat on my taxes. I can gossip my head off in the name of sharing prayer requests. I can do whatever I want. God will still love me."

That's true. God's love for you is absolutely unconditional. You didn't earn his love, and there's nothing you can do that would make God stop loving you. But are these saints enjoying peace on earth? They clearly have a lot more free time on their hands (since they're not micromanaging the planet), and quite frankly, I think they're more fun to be around. But no, indeed, they haven't found peace either. Instead, they are wracked with guilt and an uneasy feeling that, even though they're "getting away with something" because Jesus is their free ticket to heaven, deep inside they know they were meant for higher living. Their spirits groan under the weight of all their sin.

The Bible says we are not under law but under grace:

> What shall we say, then? Shall we go on sinning so that grace may increase? By no means! We died to sin; how can we live in it any longer?
>
> Romans 6:1–2

As I meditated on the Scriptures concerning peace, what jumped out at me was how often Peace and Righteousness were linked. Only when you live right, when your conscience is clear before God, can you enjoy peace. To me, the epitome of the tranquil lifestyle God

71

desires for us to experience is found in the Twenty-third Psalm.

The LORD is my shepherd, I shall not be in want.
  He makes me lie down in green pastures,
he leads me beside quiet waters,
  he restores my soul.
He guides me in paths of righteousness
  for his name's sake.
Even though I walk
  through the valley of the shadow of death,
I will fear no evil,
  for you are with me;
your rod and your staff,
  they comfort me.

You prepare a table before me
  in the presence of my enemies.
You anoint my head with oil;
  my cup overflows.
Surely goodness and love will follow me
  all the days of my life,
and I will dwell in the house of the LORD
  forever.

I am often intrigued not only by what the Bible says, but by what it *implies*. When God tells us he is our Shepherd, he is implying that we will need one. If you think about it, the only reason sheep need a shepherd is because they are surrounded by danger: not only predators who want to harm them, but hazards that are inherent in their environment such as steep cliffs or raging rivers. In addition, sheep are a hazard to themselves because they often behave foolishly and put themselves in harm's way.

We need a Shepherd because we have three enemies: the world, the flesh, and the enemy. And what does David say the Shepherd does for him? He says: "He restores my soul." He doesn't say, "He burdens me down with rules and regulations, so I can make myself and everyone around me miserable." He says, "He restores my soul." He doesn't say, "He turns me loose to get into all kinds of trouble, so I can blend right in with the heathen who surround me." He says, "He restores my soul. He guides me in paths of righteousness *for his name's sake*" (italics added).

Notice it doesn't say he leads us in paths of righteousness so we can look down our spiritual noses at everyone else or expend our energy telling everyone else how to live. It says God restores our soul so *we* can live right for his name's sake. What is his name? His reputation. So what's at stake in your life is not your eternal destiny. That's settled at the cross. That's covered by grace. What's at stake is your peace and God's reputation. In other words, whether or not your life will give the world an accurate picture of the God who so freely gave his life for you.

God wants you to experience his peace so people can look at your life and get an accurate idea of what God is all about. That's why we need God to restore our souls: our mind, will, and emotions. Perhaps more than any other area, the battle to restore our souls is waged in the mind. Oswald Chambers observed: "Our stamina is sapped, not so much through external troubles surrounding us but through problems in our thinking."[1]

In particular, you have to change the way you think about yourself. I know I've written about this before in previous books, but it is so important! Let me ask you something: How would you feel if the most important person in your life constantly said out loud to you the things you say to yourself? Half of you would be in the fetal position, unable to function.

We constantly tell ourselves rotten things about ourselves, then we wonder why we can't get a moment's peace. William Backus, author of *Telling Yourself the Truth*, explains:

> Your internal monologue is the never-silent stream of words or images running through your head night and day, the automatic thoughts that habitually pop into your head unbidden, generated automatically from your beliefs. We can know scriptural truth, yet still allow ourselves to be [negatively] influenced by untrue self-talk. All too often we *make ourselves miserable* and *keep ourselves miserable* by listening to a nonstop stream of inner nonsense [and self-defeating self-criticism]. The cause of our emotional ups and downs comes from within us—not what happens to us, but what we tell ourselves as we interpret what's happening to us. What we tell ourselves determines the quality of our lives.[2]

Most people ruminate upon the same handful of topics day after day. We are creatures of habit, even in our thinking patterns. So many of us rob ourselves of peace by focusing our minds on negative things that create emotional turmoil. I meet too many depressed Christian women who are consumed with thoughts like, "I'm a loser. I'm so fat. I'm getting old. I don't look like the women on the cover of the magazines. I'm a failure as a wife and mom. I hate my life." On and on. Negative, negative. And they wonder why they don't have any peace!

Some of you have a long history of attracting the wrong kind of people into your life. Yes, I said *attracting*.

Whether it's the wrong kind of friends or the wrong kind of boyfriends. The theological term for such people is RATS. It's from the Latin, *rottenous ratinous*. Some of you find yourself in one rotten situation after another or facing one disaster after another. Until recently, I described myself as "a weird experiences magnet." Things routinely happened to me that never happened to anyone else! People were constantly taking advantage of me, or I'd get embroiled in one mess after another. The theological term for such situations is also, conveniently enough, RATS.

Our problem is that we think the problem is the rats! It's that rotten boyfriend. That rat. We've got to get rid of him, so we fight him off with a stick. And guess what? Another one just like him comes crawling out of the woodwork. Did you ever notice that? Or you've got a rat for a boss. So you get a new job, and guess what? Your new boss is your old boss's twin brother! Or everywhere you go, you wind up with a bunch of conniving co-workers. Those rats! So you have to keep changing jobs. Or maybe there are rats at every church you attend, so you have to keep changing churches. But no matter where you go, the rat brigade is already there waiting for you.

Maybe the rats in your life are financial setbacks. Ruined friendships. Weight gain. Or chronic health problems. You are constantly fighting or fleeing rats! You know, every once in a while, someone loves you enough to serve it up straight. A pastor friend of mine, Mike Mugavero from Texas, did that for me some time ago. I was sitting at his kitchen table, pleading with him to help me fight off all these rats. He looked me dead in the eyes and said, "Donna, if you get rid of the garbage, the rats will leave." I better say that one again:

If you get rid of the garbage, the rats will leave.

Some of you have been fighting the wrong enemy all your life. You thought the problem was the rats. You thought the problem was out there. The problem is right between your ears. It's all that garbage in your head. We have met the enemy and she is us.

Ironically, the best way to get rid of the garbage is *not* to focus on the garbage, taking it out one piece at a time, studying it, trying to figure out who's to blame for putting it in there. If that approach worked, I would be Mother Teresa by now. Trust me, it doesn't work. Instead, deliberately turn your attention to the positive—and I want you to be very aggressive about it. I'm not talking about wasting your time on wishful thinking. No, I'm talking about reprogramming your mind with the truth of God's Word. Romans 12:2 says:

> Do not conform any longer to the pattern of this world, but be transformed by the renewing of your mind. Then you will be able to test and approve what God's will is—his good, pleasing and perfect will.

Someone once said that what most of us need is brainwashing, using God's Word as the soap. Here's how one dictionary defines *brainwash*: "to teach a set of ideas so thoroughly as to change a person's beliefs and attitudes completely." Sounds pretty good, doesn't it? Maybe it's time for you to get serious about washing your brain. (Incidentally, if you would like more help in the area of restoring your soul, please refer to my previous book

Someone once said that what most of us need is brainwashing, using God's Word as the soap.

Becoming the Woman I Want to Be: 90 Days to Renew Your Spirit, Soul, and Body [Bethany House, 2004].)

I've made it my goal not to turn this book into the script for a Major Motion Picture by telling you all my sob stories. However, in order for me to give you an accurate reflection of the God we serve, there are some things about my life I feel compelled to share. When God saw that I had come to the end of myself and was ready to cooperate with him as he began doing a serious work of restoring my soul, he led me to someone who specialized in counseling battered women. The counselor told me I was the most severe case he'd ever seen in twenty-plus years of practice. I don't say that for dramatic effect. But I'm telling you: I was an absolute wreck. Physically, emotionally, mentally, in every way—I was a wreck. I don't say that to elicit your pity. I don't want your pity. In fact, I don't want anything. "The LORD is my shepherd, I shall not want." Or my paraphrase: "The Lord is my shepherd, I'm not missing out on anything." I am sharing this only because I want you to know that if God can restore my soul, if I can experience peace on earth, there is hope for every woman reading these words.

He is leading me beside still waters. He's making me to lie down in green pastures. He is setting a table before me in the presence of mine enemies. Where are our enemies, by the way? Are they up in heaven? No, they're right here on earth, aren't they? God says he will prepare a table—a symbol of his abundant provision, of his absolute care for you—he will prepare a table before you in the presence of your enemies. And everyone will see with their own eyes what God can do when he *restores your soul*. When he leads you in paths of righteousness *for his name's sake*. When you can finally get a moment's peace!

Down and Out in Scorpionville

I think of all who've come before me and had to endure trials that would level most of us in our urban comfort zones, and I realize I'm not the first person to face big challenges. This has been done before. I can do it again, maybe even better.

Oprah Winfrey[1]

Do you ever feel like God is picking on you?

Or maybe you think the enemy is picking on you?

Or you know *someone* is picking on you—you're just not sure who?

Do you ever feel like Job ain't got nothing on you? I've already admitted that I used to describe myself as "a weird experiences magnet." Just to give you a small example, my annual septic system service was being done when I heard a knock on the door. There wasn't a shadow of a doubt in my mind what it was all about.

(I have those evil-surmisings down pat.) Sure enough, I opened the door in time to inhale the most delightful odor. The forlorn man on my front steps swore to the high heavens, "This has never happened to me in twenty years of cleaning septic systems, but . . ."

I stopped him midsentence, "But you're at *my* house now. That's a whole different ball game. Stuff happens to me *every day* that never happens to anyone else." Yes, indeed, I had raw sewage all over my yard. That was right after my well ran dry and I lived without running water for six weeks, right before the second-largest forest fire in American history came within twelve miles of my house. Shall I continue? I promise, I'm just getting to the good stuff.

Uh-oh. Donna's in Major Motion Picture mode!

Here's the kind of puzzling questions I routinely ponder: If God is sovereign, why is the world so out of control? If he is all-powerful, he mustn't be a very good God to allow children to be kidnapped, molested, and murdered. Why does he allow famine to strike and wars to rage? If God is love, why is there so much hatred in the world? Who am I kidding? Forget the world-at-large, if God is sovereign, why is my little world so often out of control? So filled with heartache and disappointment? If Jesus came to bring peace, health, and life, why is there so much strife, sickness, and death in the world? Where is God and what is he THINKING?

Sometimes we struggle to understand what God is up to on this planet and in our private worlds.

Let's get personal. Do you ever wonder: If God loves me, why does he apparently stand idly by and let rotten stuff happen to me? Is it okay to get this real on the pages of a Christian book? I sure hope so. I think if we were honest, we would all admit that sometimes we struggle to understand what God is up to on this planet and in our private worlds.

I want to share two recent experiences God has worked through in a profound way to teach me more about all this madness we call the human experience. And to help me through those moments when my life honestly feels like a Major Motion Picture.

In December 2002, I bought a house on the outskirts of Phoenix, Arizona. Since I am terrified of scorpions, I specifically asked *in writing* whether or not the house I was interested in buying had a scorpion problem. Of course, the owners assured me, "Not a problem." They lied. Shortly after we moved in, the teenager from across the street stopped over and remarked with great admiration, "So, you weren't afraid to move into the Scorpion House?"

My stunned response: *"The WHAT?"*

"Yeah," he calmly explained. "We call it the Scorpion House because that's where they all like to hang out. Do you want me to come over at night with my black light and see how many we can find?"

All I could think was "No, I don't want to look for scorpions. I want God to take the scorpions away." Some time later, I was walking past the rocking chair where I sit with my little prayer basket to have my morning devotions. It's my favorite place in the whole world. My refuge. My fortress. As I live and breathe, there was a *scorpion* crawling up the side of my rocking chair! I just know it was planning to burrow itself in the cushion and wait for me until morning.

No matter how hard I pray, though, I can't change the fact that we live in Scorpionville. I'm still holding out for a miracle, just so you know. But until that day, I have pledged my life to do battle against the scorpions.

81

The way I see it, it is *not* the scorpions' house. Not unless they want to start making the mortgage payments. It's my house. And I've taken it on as my assignment to fight the good fight with all the wisdom, strength, and bug people God supplies. You know what makes me smile? I know something those wretched creatures are too stupid to understand. Someday—I don't know when—but someday, I'm getting a new house somewhere nice. I don't know where, but I believe God has a special spot picked out just for me. Maybe near an ocean. Green grass. Beautiful flowers. No desert. No rattlesnakes. No scorpions.

Meanwhile, I've decided I'm going to enjoy this house. When I first moved in, I was extremely discouraged. But then I just made up my mind: as long as I'm stuck here, I'm going to make the best of it. And when I move out, those scorpions will be left behind, trapped in the Arizona desert forever. You have no idea how much joy that simple thought has brought into my life.

I don't know why God created scorpions. I think this world would be a much better place without them. I can pretend they don't exist, but that will only make them more dangerous. We have an enemy far more deadly than a scorpion. I know for a fact this world would be a much better place without the influence of the evil one, the Great Scorpion. If I were creating the universe, I wouldn't have created Satan. Nor would I have created angels capable of becoming demons. But God, whose ways are not our ways, chose to create them. And they are alive and active on planet Earth. We can pretend the Great Scorpion doesn't exist, but that will do us no good. We have to fight the battle. And if we refuse to fight, if we look the other way, the enemy will only grow in power and influence over this world.

We can get all discouraged and depressed when we look at this world "with devils filled," as Martin Luther put it. Or we can look at the bright side. Someday, we're all getting new houses in heaven. And when we do, those hate-filled creatures are going to fry in a sun-scorched land forever. Meanwhile, we've got to get a holy determination to fight the battle *and* enjoy our lives at the same time. Let's not forget the other side of the equation. Those scorpions hate me as much as I hate them. That's why they want to sting me and inject me with poison. From their perspective, they probably look at me and wonder: *Why did God create her? The big oaf. I really don't see what she contributes!* Besides, they were living in that house before I moved in. In fact, they were in this location long before the first human being set foot upon its barren soil and said, "Great location. Think I'll build a house right here."

In the same way, Satan is a hate-filled creature. And he hates you because you are a child of God. He considers this planet his home. He was here long before you showed up. He knows he can't kill you, but he'll settle for inflicting as much pain as he possibly can.

In John 10:10, Jesus said:

> The thief comes only to steal and kill and destroy; I have come that they may have life, and have it to the full.

There's a tension. Jesus wants you to have and enjoy life to the fullest; the Great Scorpion wants to steal, kill, and destroy. There's a war going on that's beyond any Major Motion Picture you've ever seen. It's Star Wars *times* infinity, and we are part of the intergalactic battle force.

> Finally, be strong in the Lord and in his mighty power. Put on the full armor of God so that you can take your

stand against the devil's schemes. For our struggle is not against flesh and blood, but against the rulers, against the authorities, against the powers of this dark world and against the spiritual forces of evil in the heavenly realms.

Ephesians 6:10–12

Satan hates you and he wants to hurt you. As long as you deny the existence of the Great Scorpion or fail to realize the magnitude of his hatred for you, your life will never make sense. You will blame God for the actions of the enemy.

Maybe I'm simpleminded, but I need to keep things simple. Here's what has helped me make sense of this world. Everything that involves stealing, killing, or destroying comes from the enemy. Period. God does not steal, kill, or destroy. James 1:13–15 explains:

When tempted, no one should say, "God is tempting me." For God cannot be tempted by evil, nor does he tempt anyone; but each one is tempted when, by his own evil desire, he is dragged away and enticed. Then, after desire has conceived, it gives birth to sin; and sin, when it is full-grown, gives birth to death.

And I think by implication, we can add for clarification: Whenever you *get stung*, when your life is under attack, when there is stealing, killing, and destruction going on—that is *not* God's handiwork. James wants to be sure we get this, so the very next verse warns:

Don't be deceived, my dear brothers. Every good and perfect gift is from above, coming down from the Father of the heavenly lights, who does not change like shifting shadows.

James 1:16–17

Again, we see the tension. God wants to bless us with every good and perfect gift, but there are scorpions on the loose. Satan wants to thwart God's good plans for you. If he can't get you in hell, he'll do everything he can to give you hell on earth. Maybe you have non-Christian friends whose lives look just peachy keen, while your life looks like a war zone. That's because the Great Scorpion knows he'll be living with them for all eternity, but *you* are moving out and moving up. He can torment them later; he's got to torment you *now*.

> Here's what has helped me make sense of this world. Everything that involves stealing, killing, or destroying comes from the enemy. Period.

The word *Satan* actually means "accuser." Way back in the Garden of Eden, Satan *accused* God of withholding good gifts from his children. His message to Eve was basically "God is holding out on you. He has all these good gifts, but he's not giving them to you. You are an underprivileged child. You better grab what you want for yourself." Satan's objective was to sow doubt in Eve's mind. He wanted her to doubt the goodness of God because he knew her doubt would automatically lead to rebellion.

We need to stop right there.

Satan wants you to doubt the goodness of God. That's his #1 goal. He thinks if he can just get you to doubt God's goodness, you will rebel. His lies and tactics never change. What was the purpose of his attacks on Job? He wanted him to "Curse God and die" as Job's wife so sweetly suggested (Job 2:9). It's the same old stuff. He spent months telling me: "Hey, Donna. God is holding out on you! Look, you're stuck in the Scorpion House while *everyone else* is living somewhere wonderful." I was totally falling for it! I finally woke up and said, "Satan, you are a liar! God is *not* holding out on me."

You need to know today that God is not holding out on you either. Don't let the Great Scorpion cause you to doubt the goodness of God. Let's go back to our two key verses:

> Every good and perfect gift is from above.
>
> James 1:17

But:

> The thief comes only to steal and kill and destroy.
>
> John 10:10

So God is about the business of giving gifts, and Satan is about the business of snatching those good gifts. There's something very personal I want to share with you, and I hope it won't sound like a Major Motion Picture. In all sincerity, I realize there are millions of people in this world whose suffering far exceeds anything I can even fathom. Nevertheless, I had a painful experience last summer that made a profound impact on my life. I was scheduled to teach a five-week series at my home church entitled "The Journey to Hope." I was indeed filled with hope—and joy—as my husband and I had discovered we were expecting a baby. We knew God had given us a precious gift. We were so thankful! But then, just two weeks before the conference began, I had a miscarriage. I delivered a tiny, eleven-week-old baby, maybe four inches long, a few ounces in weight. We named the baby Jack after my father. We buried him in our yard and planted a rose bush in remembrance of his short life.

I believe God's heart was to give us a precious gift. And he did. Jack will always be part of us. I have drawn more strength, more determination, more joy from his brief life than just about anything else I can think of. I am a changed woman. Truly.

In my previous book *This Isn't the Life I Signed Up For*, I mentioned that my sister, Helen, works with cancer patients at St. Christopher's Hospital for Children in Philadelphia. Now as far as I'm concerned, children and cancer should not be in the same sentence. But she sees it every day. My sister says—and she of all people should know—tragedy merely brings out what's already there. It doesn't make the parents stronger. If they are strong, they survive. If they aren't strong, they fall apart. She says: "Some people blame God. Some people doubt God. The smart ones *thank* God for allowing them to experience whatever time they *did* have with their child."

What wisdom! The smart ones *thank* God for allowing them to experience whatever time they did have with their child. I'm so thankful for those few short weeks my husband and I had with Jack. It's a precious memory, and Satan can never steal that from us. I went on to write in that book (this was before we lost Jack):

I used to think hardship was the best way to build character. I was wrong. It's certainly one way, but it's not the most effective way. (Yet another brain torque for those of us who specialize in learning everything through painful experience.) The best way to build our character is in meditation upon the promises of God, convincing our hearts of his goodness. That way, if and when tragedy does strike, we will endure. And

87

this much I know for sure: two months of such meditation has done more to transform my personality than
twenty years of "look it up and find the right answer"
Bible study.

We are not transformed by rising to the occasion. We
rise to the occasion because we have been transformed.
How are we transformed? By the renewing of our mind.
*By convincing our heart that God is good, even when our
circumstances are not.*

Well, apparently the Great Scorpion had read my
book, but didn't think I really believed what I wrote. I
was about to find out for myself what I truly believed,
but first here's a thought that crossed my mind: *Where
was God when the thief came to steal, kill, and destroy?
Didn't he see him coming? Why didn't he stop him?*

I must tell you, when I asked God that question, his
answer was so clear I simply couldn't miss it. I find that
when God speaks to me, he speaks Scripture. And here
is what he said to me:

Satan has asked to sift you as wheat. But I have prayed
for you, that your faith may not fail. And when you have
turned back, strengthen your sisters.

Those were the words Jesus spoke to Simon Peter in
Luke 22:31–32. Now here's what most of us would like
that verse to say: "Satan has asked to sift you as wheat,
but I told him no way! You cannot lay a hand on him."
But that's not what it says. In fact, let's read between
the lines a little bit. I think Jesus was saying:

Simon, Satan has asked to sift you as wheat. It wasn't an
easy decision for me, but I've decided, in this particular
instance, to let him go ahead and do it. I have such an
important assignment for you. There is no way you can
do what I'm calling you to do until you master certain

lessons. My heart's desire was to teach you every single one of them the easy way. That's why I spent three years with you. You've come far, but you've got farther to go. Those things you failed to learn sitting at my feet, now you must learn the hard way, as the Enemy sifts you like wheat. But I'm praying for you, and I know you'll make it through. When you do, use what you've learned to strengthen your brothers.

That is precisely what I believe God wanted to say to me. And I believe it's what he wants to say to some of you. God's desire is for us to learn our lessons the easy way, sitting at Jesus's feet. He doesn't want our life to provide enough dramatic material to constitute a Major Motion Picture. Unfortunately, some of us just won't sit still long enough, so we end up learning the hard way, as Satan sifts us like wheat.

I believe God has a specific assignment for every Christian. Along with that assignment, he has prepared a specific course of study for your life. There are certain prerequisites that must be fulfilled before you can move to the next level of service and usefulness in his kingdom. Now, if you just want to sit in a pew, Satan won't sift you much. But then again, your life won't count for much either.

But make no mistake about this: the more significant the assignment you are willing to take on, the tougher the course of study God will require. And God will give you one opportunity after another to "get it"—to master the lessons. Did you ever notice how the same stuff keeps happening to you? Or you keep finding yourself in situations that elicit the same response? And you think, *Why does this stuff keep happening to me?* Why? Because you still don't "get it." When you finally "get it," you can take a different class. Of course, it will probably be an even harder class, but at least it won't be the same old, same old.

As I've already confessed, my particular class was "Weird Experiences 101." Despite my years of Bible study and profound theological insights, it never even occurred to me that God was standing there the whole time saying, "HELLO!!! Could you please just get this one so we can *move on*? Because we can't *move on* until you get it!"

I'm embarrassed to admit this, but I flunked that same dumb test every single time! Every time something weird would happen, the first thing I would do was question the goodness of God. I'd pitch a pity party. I'd whine and complain to anybody who would listen. Now when I look back, it's painfully obvious that God allowed Satan to keep turning up the heat. Things moved from "weird" to "worse." The enemy attacked my car, my house, my friendships, my finances, my health, my ministry, and my personal life. And almost without exception, I flunked that dumb test every time.

But then, the enemy overplayed his hand. He pushed it too far. I'm convinced losing our baby was the biggest miscalculation the enemy ever made in my life. He figured I'd pitch another of my famous pity parties. "God doesn't really love me. God's picking on me again. Why does he let this stuff keep happening to me?" That's exactly where I was headed. Within an hour of delivering our baby, I was sitting beside my husband, sobbing hysterically. I started screaming at the top of my lungs: "Why, God? Why? Why does this stuff keep happening to me? Why? Why? Why?"

Then something just came over me. I believe it was the power of the Holy Spirit. I literally stood up and said, "No, devil, No. You are not going to take me down over this." And I knew with everything that was within me. I knew like I had never known before:

God is good . . . even when my circumstances are not.

I knew at that moment, down to the very core of my being, that those were the truest words I had ever spoken. I'm convinced that strength came from the countless hours I had spent meditating on God's Word, meditating on the goodness of God. My heart is finally convinced within me: God is good. As Job said, "Though he slay me, yet will I trust in him" (Job 13:15 KJV). I knew that I knew that every good gift I've ever enjoyed, every good thing that's ever happened in my life was directly from his hand. I knew:

God is good . . . even when my circumstances are not.

Do you know that? The enemy is the one who comes to steal, kill, and destroy. Satan and his minions were behind every rotten thing that has ever happened to you and to me. And the enemy better look out now because I *get it*. I finally *GET IT*. I'll tell you another thing. I'm on a mission to make sure the enemy pays full price for every item he has ever stolen from me. And I believe at this very moment, even as I write these words, even as you read these words, he is paying! Because I know some of you finally *get it*. Wake up! The enemy is the one who comes to steal your joy, kill your dreams, and destroy your life.

The church has an anger problem. Not that we're too angry. We're not angry enough. We need to get good and angry. Except we need to get angry at the right one—not angry at our parents, not angry at our husbands, not angry at our co-workers or our pastor, not angry at our circumstances, and certainly not angry at God, who has never done anything except bless us. We need to get good and angry at the enemy. That Great Scorpion. And we ought to devote our lives to crushing him under our feet. That's where the Bible says he belongs. Some of you need to rise up and declare, "Devil, you made me mad now. And I'm going to make you pay for everything you've ever done to me."

How do you make him pay? Nothing could be easier. By devoting your life to glorifying God, by being determined to fulfill God's purpose for your life. To be able to say, even as Jesus was able to say in speaking to the Father, "I have completed the work you gave me to do." You make the enemy pay by learning your lessons, passing your tests the *first time*, and by fulfilling your specific assignment in the kingdom of God.

God has a specific assignment for you. Along with that comes a specific curriculum—a set of lessons to learn and tests to pass. You have the option. You can learn your lessons the easy way, by sitting at Jesus's feet. Or you can learn the hard way, with Satan sifting you as wheat. Let's look at Option #1, shall we?

Option #1: The Easy Way—Sitting at Jesus's Feet

We sit at Jesus's feet through the spiritual disciplines of prayer, fasting, Bible study, and corporate worship, which I will cover in greater detail in the next chapter. For now, let me just say that every person reading this book needs to be in a weekly Bible study. If you're thinking, *Well, I already know all that stuff*, great. Then you should be teaching by now. I know, I know, you don't have time. Well, take it from me, learning the easy way is far less time-consuming than learning the hard way. If you honestly think you can save time by neglecting fellowship and accountability, by neglecting the systematic study of God's Word, you are seriously deceived.

When it comes to learning in God's classroom, we can't expect to graduate if we are constantly absent from school. God provides the opportunity, but we must avail ourselves of it. God will send people into your life—pastors, teachers, authors, and friends—with words to spark your spiritual growth. However, it is your responsibility to be available and willing to hear their words with an open heart. God will communicate with you through prayer, but you are responsible for setting

> When it comes to learning in God's classroom, we can't expect to graduate if we are constantly absent from school.

aside time in prayer. God will teach you through the Bible, customizing the lesson to suit your needs, but it is your responsibility to study and meditate upon his Word. God will cleanse you in the silent moments, speaking in his still, small voice, but you have to turn off the noise long enough to listen.

Some of you are thinking: *Spiritual disciplines? Sounds kind of boring. What's Option #2?* Glad you asked.

Option #2: The Hard Way—Satan Sifting You like Wheat

Before we go any further, I think it's important to emphasize that God will only let Satan sift you if there's something in your life he wants to get rid of. I hope that's of some comfort! The most basic form of sifting

93

is being around *Annoying People*. For example, I home-schooled my children for many years, and I often said, "If it weren't for my kids, I would love homeschooling. And if it weren't for homeschooling, I would probably love my kids." When I was surrounded all day long by those little sinners, they just seemed to sin all the time. But that's not the worst of it. They made *me* sin! One thing I struggle with is my thought life. Sometimes when my kids were making me crazy, I would go off into my little fantasy world. And I would dream about a man . . . in a yellow school bus taking them away. I knew if I could just ship my kids off to boarding school, I would be mother of the year. Instead, they kept making me sin! One day God said to me, "Donna, your children are not *making* you sin. They are *revealing* your sin."

Guess what? Your children are not making you sin. Your husband isn't making you sin. Your lack of a husband isn't making you sin. Your boss isn't making you sin. The people at your church aren't making you sin. *They are revealing your sin*. And furthermore, they are doing you a favor. Sin has to be dealt with in three steps, according to 1 John 1:9: "If we confess our sins, he is faithful and just to forgive us our sins, and to cleanse us of all unrighteousness" (KJV).

That's Christianity 101. God desires that we be cleansed of sin. In order for that to happen, we must confess it. But we're not going to confess it until we confront it. Think about this for a moment. Annoying people force you to:

1. Confront your sin so you can
2. Confess so God can
3. Cleanse you from it

So you see, annoying people actually perform an important public service. I have a special assignment for you. I want you to write a thank-you note to the most annoying person you know. You can be honest: *"Dear Sarah, I want to thank you for the powerful role you are playing in my spiritual growth. I cannot begin to tell you the ways God is transforming my life through my relationship with you. Sincerely, Your Sister in Christ!"*

Annoying Circumstances are the next level of Hard Way learning. I've already shared quite a bit on this particular topic, but I suspect some of you may be weird experience magnets, too. Some of you cannot go anywhere without encountering an annoying circumstance. Everywhere you go, something goes wrong: the grocery store, the movie theater, the mall. Do you always get in the slow lane everywhere you go? Do you always get the sales clerk who has no clue what she's doing? I was convinced there was a person whose sole responsibility in life was to drive ahead of me all day, putting up those orange construction-zone cones just to impede my progress.

Think about it this way: Maybe if you would sit quietly at Jesus's feet, you wouldn't end up sitting in traffic all the time, because God wouldn't have to allow so many annoying circumstances into your life!

If you still don't get it, God will allow Satan to really sift you as wheat by allowing painful trials: "Consider it pure joy, my brothers, whenever you face trials of many kinds, because you know that the testing of your faith develops perseverance" (James 1:2–3).

The truth is, some lessons can only be learned the hard way, out in the real world. I got straight A's on all my chemistry exams, but I flunked the lab portion. I was great at book knowledge, but then we had to take the next step and apply what we had learned to a real-world situation. That's when I always blew it. For some life classes, God requires us to take the laboratory component. If we remain calm and God-confident even when faced with real-world exams, we will progress through our course of study. Here's how Andrew Murray, a nineteenth-century author, described it in his book *Humility*:

> In time of trouble say,
> First, he brought me here. It is by his will I am in this place; in that will I rest.
> Next, he will keep me in his love and give me grace in this trial to behave as his child. Then, he will make the trial a blessing, teaching me the lessons he means for me to learn, and working in me the grace he intends for me. Last, in his good time, he can bring me out again, how and when only he knows. Say:
>
> I am here.
> By God's appointment,
> In God's keeping,
> Under his training,
> For his time.[2]

The Easy Way or the Hard Way. You can sit at Jesus's feet or Satan will sift you like wheat. It's up to you. Even when you learn the hard way, remember God is in the midst of it all. God will never allow Satan to sift you unless he has a specific plan in mind for how he can work that experience out for your ultimate good. Not that your pain was God's idea, but God has an idea to bring something good out of it.

One of my favorite people in the Bible is Joseph. I'm sure you remember his story. His brothers sold him into slavery. His owner's wife tried to seduce him, then falsely accused him of assaulting her. He was thrown in prison—a dungeon, really—and left to rot there for many years. The enemy was behind all of that. The hatred of his brothers, the seduction and lies of Potiphar's wife, and you can be sure Satan was busy at work in that dungeon. But God was there, too. Joseph learned some of his life lessons the hard way, but he learned them well. When he finally had opportunity to confront the brothers who caused him so much pain, he said:

> You intended to harm me, but God intended it for good to accomplish what is now being done, the saving of many lives.
>
> Genesis 50:20

God wants to give you good gifts, but he has an even higher goal for your life. I want to give good gifts to my children, but more importantly, I want to shape their character to prepare them for the rest of their lives. Only an irresponsible parent would shower children with gifts and never train or discipline them. God disciplines his children because he loves us. He wants to prepare us for service in his kingdom—both here on the earth and in the kingdom that is coming.

The enemy is always meddling with your circumstances, and God obviously gives him some room to do it. Why? Because God is always focused on your character and your future: "an eternal glory that far outweighs them all" (2 Cor. 4:17).

The movie *Out of Africa* contains an interesting scene where Karen Blixen has just arrived in Kenya from Denmark and is completely clueless about life on the savannah. She is out walking, unarmed, when a lioness confronts her. As she stands there terror-struck, a wise hunter happens upon her and offers this advice from shouting distance: "Don't run, Baroness, or she'll think you're something good to eat." Baroness Blixen stares the lion right in the eyes, stands her ground, and sure enough, the lion walks away.

Yes, we have an enemy roaming around like a roaring lion, actively seeking someone to devour. But if we simply stand firm in the face of his attacks, he'll go roar somewhere else. We have God's Word on that: Resist the devil, and he *will* flee from you (James 4:7, italics added). We don't need to become obsessed with him, but neither should we ignore him. We should see him for the roaring lion he is and respond accordingly: Don't run. Stand firm.

How on Earth Am I Supposed to Find Time for God?

"I'm late. I'm late. For a very important date. I'm late, I'm late, I'm late," said the white rabbit in *Alice in Wonderland*.

I want to pick up where I left off in the last chapter with the issue of learning our life lessons the easy way, rather than the hard way (also known as the Major Motion Picture way). Too many of us live at a frenzied pace, trying to be all things to all people. Some of you are still trying to raise your children, and now your parents have become like little children. You're part of the Sandwich Generation, caught between competing allegiances and obligations. In between running Jason back and forth from school to basketball games and getting Katie to band practice on time, you have to take your mother to her umpteenth doctor's appointment of the month.

Or your grown children are acting like children, so now you have to raise their children just when you thought you were done with parenting.

Maybe you're a working mother, torn between the demands of your boss and the needs of your family. Or you're a stay-at-home mom struggling to survive on one income in a two-income world. You spend half the day chasing kids and the other half clipping coupons and running to three different grocery stores in a desperate attempt to save $15.

The only time you sit still long enough to ponder the madness of your Emmy award–worthy personal drama is Sunday mornings, when the pastor has the nerve to lecture you on the importance of a daily quiet time. *Please! Who is he kidding?* Even if you could get your life to STOP for about five seconds, you wouldn't be able to spend that time reading the Bible because you'd be in shock! The only women who have daily quiet times are the ones with husbands who earn six-figure incomes. They're also the only ones bursting with enough energy to leap out of bed in the morning, because they have a personal trainer and spend their free time taking tennis lessons and getting facials.

But real women haven't got time for God. The whole world *needs* us right *now,* and if we don't personally handle everything ourselves *right now* it won't get done and the world will fall apart. I love the line from Sara Groves's song "How Is It Between Us":

When I wake up I am on my way
Reinventing the wheel
And saving the day!

In case you've forgotten, the wheel has already been invented, so there's no need to exhaust yourself trying to reinvent it. But that doesn't stop people from doing it anyway! How many of us spend *hours* every day doing things that don't need to be done or doing things that could just as easily be done *by someone else?* We are indispensable! Or so we think. Can I ask you something? How is it possible that you are more indispensable than the Son of God? How is it possible that when Jesus walked the earth he somehow managed to find time to spend time with his heavenly Father, but we are far too busy, too important to set aside our agenda for thirty minutes? Perspective, sisters. Putting your problems and your daily demands into perspective. That's what this book is all about. Let's watch the disciples as they try to sweep Jesus up into Major Motion Picture mode:

> Very early in the morning, while it was still dark, Jesus got up, left the house and went off to a solitary place, where he prayed. Simon and his companions went to look for him, and when they found him, they exclaimed: "Everyone is looking for you!"
>
> Mark 1:35–37

Everyone was looking for Jesus? *Everyone?* No doubt, thousands of people were looking for him . . . but not *everyone.* See how melodrama just spirals out of control? Wasn't it dramatic enough that thousands of people were looking for Jesus? The disciples had to blow it up to even larger proportions. They had to "find him" (as if he were lost) and exclaim (as if he didn't know): "The entire planet is looking for you!"

I'm sure you're a wonderful, well-grounded woman, and I don't mean to hurt your feelings. But I do want to give you a serious and bracing reality check: *everyone* is not looking for you. *Everyone* does not need you. The Brownie Troupe is not going to collapse if you resign as den mother. The church is not going to fall apart if you take a year off from teaching Bible study. Your children

101

are not going to die if they eat peanut butter and jelly sandwiches for dinner one night a week.

I hasten to add that it should be all-natural peanut butter on whole-wheat bread. I add that because I once received a letter from a woman who was deeply concerned because *Focus on the Family* magazine had featured a picture of my family, along with an article I wrote entitled "When Daddy Is Out of Work." Get ready for the shocker: I was serving my kids sandwiches *and potato chips*! She wasn't the least bit concerned that my husband had been unemployed or underemployed for five years, but that whole potato chip scenario just put her over the top.

If Jesus, who came to earth to save the world, could take time off from his job of preaching good news to the poor, feeding the hungry, healing the sick, and raising the dead, I'm sure you can take a break, too. In fact, I bet we could find a dozen of your friends and relatives who would rise up and exclaim, "I wish that woman would give it a break!" If we would just listen to God and follow where he leads, we would soon discover that he clears a path before us. "Whether you turn to the right or to the left, your ears will hear a voice behind you, saying, 'This is the way; walk in it'" (Isa. 30:21). God will send the right people and opportunities our way. He will literally arrange "chance" encounters with the *very people* who have the answers we would otherwise end up frantically looking for to no avail.

Just as a small example, a few weeks ago I felt myself careening into Major Motion Picture mode over my daughter's upcoming school concert. I just *had* to call the teacher in charge, and I *urgently needed* to tell her that Leah was unprepared to perform the two songs she was slated to play. I was doing everything I could on the home front by relentlessly tormenting her to practice, but I had to cover all the bases. I called the teacher's home a dozen times over the course of two weeks, but she (very intelligent woman that she is) apparently keeps her phone off the hook. Of course, since I could never find her phone number when I *needed it*, I *had to* spend ten minutes tracking it down and screaming at my kids every time I remembered to call. How could I possibly fit in my quiet time when I had to *save the day*!?!

Now this is a true story. One morning, I crawled out of bed determined to spend time with God, so I sat down in my rocking chair. My daughter was running late, but for once, I didn't go nuts. Instead, I calmly drove her to school. Lo and behold, the teacher in question was sitting alone reading a book. This is an understaffed Christian school, friends. I have never, before or since, seen one of the teachers sitting undisturbed during school hours. But there she sat. I began to tell her about the impending catastrophe, but she smiled politely and looked at my daughter, who said calmly, "I'll be ready." At which point I returned sheepishly to my car. As for the rest of the story, my daughter stepped up to the piano the next night and performed two beautiful piano solos. Well, thank God I was on hand to reinvent the wheel.

Would it astound you to discover that God knows what you need before you know you need it? Does that sound too difficult for God? What is more, God knows what your husband, your children, and your church need. It gets even better. He not only knows your needs, but you can have complete confidence that he is *both able and eager* to fill those needs, according to his riches in glory. That's why Jesus said:

And when you pray, do not keep on babbling like pagans, for they think they will be heard because of their many words. Do not be like them, for your Father knows what you need before you ask him.

This, then, is how you should pray:

103

Our Father in heaven,
hallowed be your name,
your kingdom come,
your will be done
   on earth as it is in heaven.
Give us today our daily bread. . . .

Matthew 6:7–11

God knows what you need before you need it. Now, let's combine this with our key verse from the last chapter and see what we can come up with:

Every good and perfect gift is from above.

James 1:17

So we serve a God who knows what we need *and* delights in giving good gifts to his children. I have come to believe the best analogy for prayer is the one proposed by Andrew Murray back in the 1800s:

Prayer is simply the gathering of gifts.

Through prayer, we enter into the throne room of God, where he is waiting with good gifts he longs to give. We approach the throne of grace with confidence (Heb. 4:16), and God fills our arms with gifts for us, for those we love, and for the world at large. Only when we have spent time gathering gifts in the Throne Room will we have something of genuine value to offer the people we encounter each day.

If you are anything like most Christians, your prayer life isn't exactly an exciting adventure. Of course you pray. But is prayer the *one thing* you'd rather do than almost anything else? I believe it can be, once you discover what prayer is all about. In all probability, you have a prayer list. You look around and make notes

104

concerning problems you see in the world, starting with yourself and your personal needs, but then expanding to include your family, friends, and neighbors, and perhaps you even pray for the world. There's nothing inherently wrong with that. However, sometimes prayer lists can actually become an obstacle to authentic prayer.

We *think* we know what people need, but we really don't. That's why our prayer lists are often nothing more than our own agenda: at best, educated guesses, and at worst, a list of demands. I know of a woman who prayed for several years, asking God to send godly friends for her teenage daughter. Now that sounds like a reasonable prayer request, doesn't it? Godly friends would be the perfect gift for any teenage girl. Yet day after day, year after year, that prayer remained unanswered. When that young girl reached womanhood, she told her mother, "*Jesus* is my very best friend." So it turns out

> Only when we have spent time gathering gifts in the Throne Room will we have something of genuine value to offer.

that God alone knew what that teenage girl genuinely needed. What a big surprise! If this were a Major Motion Picture, that ending would be quite a twist!

You may think your husband deserves a promotion, but God knows he needs to recognize it's time to leave that job because God has something better in mind. Or your husband is not being promoted because he has character flaws God wants to transform. The sooner "the sifting" is accomplished, the sooner you'll have a better husband (that's your *other* prayer request, right?). You may even think *you* deserve a promotion, but reread the paragraph.

Our prayer lists can be helpful, but sometimes they stand in the way. If you learn nothing else from this book, I want you to remember this:

God is the one with the prayer list.

That's right. The real prayer list is the one God keeps in heaven. Just as you desire to share your prayer list with him, he desires to share his prayer list with you. Indeed, 2 Chronicles 16:9 says:

> The eyes of the LORD range throughout the earth to strengthen those whose hearts are fully committed to him.

God is actively looking for people who will set aside their own prayer lists and instead, listen intently for his voice so he can share his heart with them. That's what Jesus meant when he instructed us to pray to the Father, "Your kingdom come, your will be done."

The next time you pray, why not take out a blank piece of paper and say, "Father, what's on your prayer list today? What good gifts do you desire to give to your people?" But be careful. It may turn out that God wants to pitch a party for someone you think he should punish. Can you handle that? I love Luke 15:31, where the father says to the dutiful older brother (in the parable of the prodigal son), "You are always with me, and *everything I have* is yours" (italics added).

You may recall the older brother made himself miserable *working* for his father, but obviously didn't understand what his father was all about. Are you, by any chance, living like the older brother? If so, I'd like to interrupt your regularly scheduled Major Motion Picture to give you a news flash: the entire planet—everyone and everything on it—is at God's disposal. It's not like he's strapped for cash or running short on time. God can handle your problems far better than you can. However, God will *not* handle your problems as long as you are still on the job.

Martin Luther put it this way: "I have so much to do today I shall have to spend the first three hours in prayer." I believe one of the most powerful, life-changing, Major Motion Picture mode–destroying actions we can take is to cultivate spiritual disciplines in our lives. Twenty-five years ago, Richard Foster wrote a phenomenal book called *Celebration of Discipline.* Many Americans probably look at that title and say, "HUH? Why would you celebrate discipline? How is discipline something to celebrate?" Discipline has a negative connotation for most of us. Discipline means a spanking, a punishment.

> If we are to make disciples of others, we should begin by making disciples of ourselves.

But discipline is the essence of being a disciple. According to the dictionary, a disciple is "a learner; a student; one who receives instruction from another." Jesus didn't say, "Go make converts." He didn't say, "Get people to make decisions for Christ." He said, "Make disciples." If we are to make disciples of others, we should begin by making disciples of ourselves.

Am I starting to make you nervous? Is this sounding like another lecture on the importance of a daily quiet time? Stick with me and I promise to reward you with a gift in the end. One of the greatest Christian authors of the modern era was Father Henri Nouwen, a Dutch priest of keen intellect and rare spiritual insight. He observed:

Discipline is the human effort to create the space in which God can be generous and give you what you need.[1]

If that doesn't bless your socks off, I'm out of ideas. We read God's Word, we fast and pray, we attend corporate worship. Why? To make room in our lives for God to *freely give us what we need* . . . and so much more! How do we make room for that to happen? I'd like to suggest three things:

1. By creating the physical space
2. By clearing out the rubble
3. By living like a disciple

Creating the Physical Space

First, we create the space for God to bless us by setting up a physical place to meet with him. But before I tell you how to do that, let me illustrate why it's so important. When I moved to my cabin in the mountains in 1998, I brought along two very stupid dogs that I called Stinker and Dinker. I occasionally went so low as to call them Dumb and Dumber. Even though we were surrounded by twenty acres of uninhabited land, my dogs liked to run out into the road. Now, if I were a dog, I'd like to run around the woods and chase rabbits and quail. Unfortunately, my dogs preferred standing in the middle of the road. And since they were exceedingly dumb, it never occurred to them that they should get out of the road when a car came along.

Apparently, the fact that my dogs were creating a dirt-road version of a traffic jam did not amuse some of my neighbors. They repeatedly kidnapped my dogs and turned them over to the local authorities. Eventually, I had no choice but to put the dogs in a cage. They barked day and night, but never realized that it was their own folly that ruined their freedom. It was their insistence on running to the wrong place that got them into trouble.

I think that's what gets us into trouble, too. We run to the wrong place. Then when we find ourselves in cages of our own creation, we bark at our circumstances and the people around us. We even bark at God. There is a better way to live.

This is what the LORD says:

"Stand at the crossroads and look;
    ask for the ancient paths,
ask where the good way is, and walk in it,
    and you will find rest for your souls."

Jeremiah 6:16

Will you stand at the crossroads of your life today and look? Will you be honest with yourself about where you are and how you got there? Once and for all, stop blaming everyone and everything else and face the person in the mirror. Will you be humble enough to seek God, asking him to show you another way to live? And when God shows you the good way, will you determine to walk in it? If so, God offers you a promise instead of a cage. You will find rest for your soul:

My soul finds rest in God alone;
    my salvation comes from him.
He alone is my rock and my salvation;
    he is my fortress, I will never be shaken.

Psalm 62:1–2

109

A fortress is the place you run to during tough times. It's the place where you feel safe.

Where do you run during tough times? Where do you run when you're depressed? When you're angry with someone? When someone has hurt your feelings? When you feel defeated and discouraged? Since I'm being bold enough to ask you such questions, let me go ahead and answer for myself. It is not unusual for me to run to food. (I'll share the other place I used to run in the next section.) When I say food, I don't mean fruits and vegetables. Over the course of many years, I developed the habit of running to my favorite junk foods: cookies, ice cream, candy bars, especially when someone hurt my feelings. I've gotten much better in recent years, but I've still got far to go on this.

I was out for my morning walk one day when I started playing around with Psalm 62. Instead of God being my fortress, I substituted my favorite comfort foods:

My soul finds rest in chocolate chip cookies alone;
　　my salvation comes from chocolate chip cookies.
Chocolate chip cookies alone are my rock and my
　　salvation;
Chocolate chip cookies are my fortress, I will never be
　　shaken.

Try it for yourself and you'll realize how ridiculous we can be. Just fill in the blanks with the place *you* run to for comfort:

My soul finds rest in ＿＿＿＿＿＿＿＿ alone;
　　my salvation comes from ＿＿＿＿＿＿＿＿.
＿＿＿＿＿＿ alone are my rock and my salvation;
　　＿＿＿＿＿＿ are my fortress, I will never be shaken.

Your first step toward creating the space in which God can be generous and give you what you need is building a fortress—a safe, healthy place you can run to. Not only when you are in trouble, but to prevent yourself from getting into trouble in the first place. Choose somewhere in your house to transform into a prayer oasis or spiritual fortress. It could be an entire room or just a corner. It could be on your front porch or in your backyard. Just find a location, then make it that place you run to, the place where you feel the safest, the most contented. And you will run there instead of running out into the middle of the road—that place that gets you into trouble, whether it's the refrigerator, the television, or the Internet.

My house is a perpetual wreck, but my prayer room is always neat, and I've tried to make it the most beautiful, inviting room in the house. The walls are painted a warm color. Lovely Victorian pictures on the wall. Flower arrangements. A little table covered in white lace with a waterfall and candle on top. Every bouquet of roses my husband has ever bought me is now dried out and hanging in my prayer room. I have two rocking chairs and my prayer basket containing my Bible, prayer journal, and the devotional book I'm currently reading. I spend time in my prayer room because it feeds my spirit.

The women in my 90-Day Renewal program who have taken up the challenge to create a fortress say it has transformed their lives. Rather than an attitude that says, "Well, I *have to* have my daily quiet time," focus on the positive. Focus on what you can do, rather than what you "have to" or are "not allowed" to do. You can create a prayer oasis—your own personal fortress. You *get to* spend time nurturing your spirit there. Isn't that better than saying, "I'm not allowed to watch TV"? It's "Hey, I'm a grown woman and I can do whatever I want to do. I choose to nurture my soul and spirit. I'm spending time in my prayer oasis because it's my favorite place

111

to be!" Let's try Psalm 62, this time substituting *prayer place*, and see how much better it works:

> My soul finds rest in my prayer place;
>   my salvation comes from my prayer place.
> My prayer place is my rock and my salvation;
>   my prayer place is my fortress, I will never be shaken.

Create a fortress for yourself! Then, the next time you need a place to run to, you'll not only have a safe place to go, you'll be creating the space in which God can be generous and give you what you need.

Clearing Out the Rubble

Second, we create space for God to bless us by clearing out the rubble in our lives. This past year, I experienced a tremendous personal revival while writing a book based on the life of Nehemiah, who returned to Jerusalem with a group of people for the express purpose of rebuilding the city walls. As much as I'd love to recount everything God taught me through that process, I shall have to content myself with two things that stand out most vividly:

> Meanwhile, the people in Judah said, "The strength of the laborers is giving out, and there is so much rubble that we cannot rebuild the wall."
>
> Nehemiah 4:10

Before they could rebuild the walls, they had to clear out the rubble. Before God can rebuild your life, you may have to clear out some rubble, too. Proverbs 25:28 says, "Like a city whose walls are broken down is a man who lacks self-control." The walls for us are spiritual disciplines. Before we can rebuild them, before we can devote ourselves to having a daily quiet time, it may be that we need to clear out some rubble. Maybe you need to clear out the rubble in your pantry. Or your refrigerator. Maybe you need to clear out the rubble in your video/DVD collection or your book and music collection. Maybe you need to clear out the rubble in your television viewing or Internet habits. Maybe you need to clear out the rubble in your head.

Something to think about anyway. Now for the real kicker:

> Eliashib the priest had been put in charge of the storerooms of the house of our God. He was closely associated with Tobiah, and he had provided him with a large room formerly used to store the grain offerings and incense and temple articles, and also the tithes of grain, new wine and oil prescribed for the Levites, singers and gatekeepers, as well as the contributions for the priests.
>
> But while all this was going on, I was not in Jerusalem, for in the thirty-second year of Artaxerxes king of Babylon I had returned to the king. Some time later I asked his permission and came back to Jerusalem. Here I learned about the evil thing Eliashib had done in providing Tobiah a room in the courts of the house of God. I was greatly displeased and threw all Tobiah's household goods out of the room. I gave orders to purify the rooms, and then I put back into them the equipment of the house of God, with the grain offerings and the incense.
>
> Nehemiah 13:4–9

When I first read this, I was puzzled. Why did Nehemiah go bonkers over just one room in the massive temple? But then I remembered that Tobiah was the

113

sworn enemy of the Israelites and had actively opposed their rebuilding program. God is showing us something here! We are the temple of the Holy Spirit, and *just one room is all it takes* to give the enemy a powerful foothold in our lives. Many Christian women have *just one room* filled with rubble—and they have no idea that *just one room* is all it takes to rob them of a vibrant relationship with God.

Let me tell you about my *one room* and the damage done. When I was in seventh grade, we had an excellent basketball team thanks in large measure to a blond-haired, green-eyed boy named Jimmy. Now it so happens that I was madly in love with Jimmy. It also happens that Jimmy did not even know I was alive, which left me feeling rejected and unloved. One Saturday afternoon, as I sat in the bleachers cheering for Jimmy, my mind wandered off to a place where Jimmy was madly in love with me and life was beautiful.

In that moment, I had inadvertently turned over *just one room* to the enemy of my soul. Rather than creating space for God to bless me, I had created a room that would lead to my destruction. It became the place I ran to whenever real life disappointed me. The place where I was the most beautiful, sought-after girl in the world. A place where no one could reject me or hurt me. It was my fortress and my hiding place. Over the years, I created a series of romantic episodes—I called them my videos—and whenever I was in pain, I would go to that room in my head and play one of the videos. It seemed so harmless.

Until the day God asked me to surrender my "video collection." I was momentarily terror-struck. I couldn't believe he would even ask such a thing. I wrestled in prayer for more than an hour, but I could not bring myself to let go. "Where will I go to be pretty?" I cried out over and over again. "Where will I go to be loved? Where will I go?" I clutched the invisible videos to my heart, rocking like a frightened child, and literally couldn't give them up. Giving up my cocaine addiction twenty-some years earlier had been *nothing* compared to this. I couldn't bear the thought of life without my videos. They were my friends! They helped me through the day! Why should I give them up? They weren't that bad. If my videos were made into Major Motion Pictures, they would have been rated PG-13 at the worst. Besides, I felt entitled to my little fantasies, because my real world was so filled with pain.

What was the harm? That's the question I was challenged to confront. How much damage had the videos done? It turns out: immeasurable. In the beginning, I only needed an occasional video to get me through the week. But as my life became increasingly painful, I needed daily videos. Then hourly videos. Eventually, it reached the point where I would spend entire days in *just one room* watching my videos and would only pay an occasional visit to the real world.

I thought the videos were my friends. I thought they were helping me cope, but they were secretly robbing me. They were a tool of the enemy for my destruction! They were robbing my children of their mother's focused attention. Robbing my friends of companionship and the positive spiritual input I should have been providing. More to the point, every time I ran to the videos I was running away from God. I was running in the wrong direction. I should have been running to my spiritual fortress to spend time with God. I should have been running to my prayer room, not my video room!

Nevertheless, I was deeply offended when a counselor told me I would need to undertake a 12-step program to help conquer my addiction. I, Donna Partow, who had been instantly delivered from drugs? Now you tell me

115

I need to work a 12-step program for this trifling little hobby? Then it became real to me. I ran to my videos for the same exact reasons I had snorted cocaine: for comfort in the midst of stressful situations, to feel desirable, invincible, to escape, to anesthetize the pain.

Why do you run to that *one room?*

Funny, I had all the time in the world to run to my videos but couldn't find time for morning devotions. Is the devil a deceiver or what? I honestly thought my videos alleviated stress, but in fact they created stress because I spent countless hours in that one room, then had to pack my real-life responsibilities into the time remaining. No wonder I was on the run! I called them my videos, and I didn't think God really minded all that much. But that's not what God called them. He called them lust and he forbade it, because he knew that even though my videos felt good for a moment, eventually they would destroy me. That's why his Word says,

> For everything in the world—the cravings of sinful man, the lust of his eyes and the boasting of what he has and does—comes not from the Father but from the world.
>
> 1 John 2:16

I am so embarrassed to admit this stuff to the world. It's not like I enjoy being an open book, you know! As a friend recently pointed out, "Basically, you are a one-woman soap opera. People buy your books because they can't wait to tune in for the next episode." But the plain truth is this: just one room was enough to rob me of the blessings God wanted to shower on me. Just one room was enough to nearly destroy my life. I wondered why my life was such a wreck; why I was so stressed-out all the time; why all my weeping and pleading with God, and all my Bible study and times of prayer and fasting, were not as effective as I would have hoped. All along, it was *just one room*.

I never intended to write about my videos; God just took over the keyboard late one night and the truth spilled out. If you think you're shocked, I'm more shocked. I had never even told my closest friends about this battle. This was God's idea, not mine. So I'm guessing that there are thousands of women who need to hear this message. Are you one of them? If so, it's time to clear out the rubble. It's time to close the door on that room and flee instead to your spiritual fortress. Ask God to show you areas of disobedience in your life where you are in violation of his divine laws. All it takes is *just one room*.

Living like a Disciple

Third, we create space for God to bless us by living like a disciple—by being one who *learns by listening*.[2] The word *listen* in Latin is *audire* (pronounced ow-DEE-ra). If you listen with great attention, the words are *ob audire*, which is where our word "obedience" comes from. So obedience literally means, "to listen with great attention." Jesus said, "If you love me, you will obey what I command" (John 14:15). It's one of the most misunderstood phrases he ever uttered. People read it as if Jesus were saying, "If you love me, you will *prove* it by obeying me. You'll run around like a chicken with your head cut off and work yourself into an early grave." That's not what he meant at all. Jesus is saying, "Focus on loving me and the obedience will take care of itself."

Let me ask you something: how did you fall in love with your husband? I suspect long conversations had something to do with it. Wasn't it as he *told you* how much he loved you, how special and beautiful he thought you were? Wasn't it as he *whispered* sweet promises

117

in your ear? You fell in love with your husband as you listened and let him share his heart with you.

As you *listen with great attention* to God, he will tell you how much he loves you, how special and beautiful he thinks you are. He will whisper sweet promises and shower you with gifts. When you *listen with great attention* to God, you can't help falling in love with him. And when you love someone, you *want* to please him. You *want* to obey him. I can honestly say I have never once had an issue with "obeying" my husband. Why would I? He loves me and only wants the best for me. He would never ask me to do anything that wasn't for my good. When you fall in love with God, you will obey God.

Now it gets interesting: If you are not listening, the Latin word is *surdus*. To not listen at all, to be completely deaf, is *absurdus*. You guessed it. That's where we get our word *absurd*. The absurd life is a life in which you are *not listening*. Is your life absurd? To not make time to listen to God, to not create the space in which God can bless you and give you what you need, *that* is absurd. That's just flat-out crazy!

> The Christian life is either a great adventure or it is nothing at all.

We practice the spiritual disciplines so we can listen and so Jesus can impart life to us. Jesus came that you might have life abundantly. He wants you to be fully alive. St. Irenaeus said, "The Glory of God is man fully alive."

Are you spiritually alive? Does your Christian faith energize you? If the Presbyterians got it right—and I think they did—then "The chief aim of man is to glorify God" (from the Westminster Shorter Catechism). If the whole reason we are on this planet is to glorify him—*glorify* means to give an accurate reflection—then we must become fully alive, fully energized by his Spirit.

What would *fully alive* look like for you? Would it be a dramatic departure from your current life of *mere existence* or *barely surviving*? Is God's Word living and active in you? When you open its pages, do the words leap out at you? Does your heart skip a beat as you read? Do you long to hear the proclamation of God's Word? Would you rather hear a sermon than watch a movie? Would you rather read your Bible than *People* magazine? Would you rather memorize Scripture than rehearse your husband's faults?

The Christian life is either a great adventure or it is nothing at all. If your religion consists of a set of doctrinal beliefs and behavioral standards, it is nothing at all. If the spiritual disciplines you've been practicing are not bringing life, something's wrong. It means you are not really *listening* to God; you're just going through the motions. You have a form of religion that denies the power of God. That kind of approach to the Christian life is *absurd*.

I have lived the Christian life both ways and, frankly, there is no comparison. I've lived the absurd life—one controlled by a sense of duty. Now, I'm living *fully alive*, simply listening to his voice and going where he leads. Truly, his yoke is easy and his burden is light.

Imagine if, rather than people avoiding you like a porcupine, they couldn't *wait* to see you coming each day. What if people leaped for joy when they saw your name on their caller ID rather than pretending they weren't at home? When you routinely spend time gathering gifts in the Father's Throne Room, people will soon figure out you are a woman with an armload of gifts to share. People will start *falling all over themselves* to be near you and to help you. I've experienced it myself. Suddenly, you'll have plenty of extra time on your hands . . . and if

119

I were you, I'd spend every minute of it gathering even more gifts from the Throne Room.

No time for God? Don't be absurd! Instead, invest the time to create the space in which God can be generous and give you what you need.

Okay, So You Had a Lousy Childhood

No one in the history of the world could possibly have had a worse childhood than mine.

You've probably already guessed that sentence is not really true, which is why it's quite remarkable that it took me forty years to figure it out. I knew there was something seriously wrong with me, but since I wasn't open to the idea that I was just a self-consumed jerk, I had to explore other possibilities. There had to be some other explanation for my wacky behavior. Thanks to Freud et al., looking for someone to blame in my childhood seemed like a productive path.

No doubt about it, if you are messed up, can't keep a job, or your phone never rings, you need answers. And it's best to begin in the beginning. There's so much material to work with. For starters, our childhoods are largely shaped by other people's choices: parents, siblings, teachers, peers, relatives, babysitters, pastors, politicians, even pedophiles. There's a whole army of people who shape our little worlds. Ergo, nothing is our fault and everything is someone else's fault. Okay, I can work with that. Chief among those other people were your parents. And if they fell an inch short of the media-created ideal, you've got the makings of a Major Motion Picture on your hands.

There's nothing like a lousy childhood to launch a great story. Think about it: Almost all the books and movies we love begin with a wretched beginning: Heidi is orphaned; so are the Little Princess and Anne of Green Gables. Almost every Shirley Temple movie features Shirley as a child in peril, either orphaned or dragged away from her only caretaker (*Bright Eyes, Captain January, Curly Top, Susannah of the Mounties*, to name a few). The Little Women endure the privations of war and separation from their father who is serving in the Union army during the American Civil War.

But what moves us is *not* these young ladies' predicaments, but their response to those predicaments. The one-sentence summaries provided by Internet booksellers are quite informative. Dover Publications provides this description of the classic movie *The Little Princess*: "Left penniless and at the mercy of a vindictive headmistress when her father dies, Sara prevails through pluck, optimism, imagination." Meanwhile, on the pages of *Anne of Green Gables*, "Anne's goodwill, intelligence, and joie de vivre ultimately endear her to her friends and neighbors as well as readers everywhere."

> There's nothing like a lousy childhood to launch a great story.

The Secret Garden portrays "a spoiled and sickly orphan [who] blossoms into a creature of loving kindness."

Somehow, I missed the point that it was their gracious response that endeared these characters to our hearts. Instead I focused on the melodrama, thinking that was the key to gaining love and attention. I figured if I could blow my stories up to Major Motion Picture status, people would care about me, too. People would want to hear my story; they'd have compassion on me and give me the coveted benefit of the doubt.

As one woman put it, "Why don't I change? Probably so I can keep on telling my sob story. If someone can just see all the pain I have had to endure all my life, then . . . then what? Somehow I think it would all be vindicated if everyone knew what everyone had done to me." That's exactly how I felt and why I never changed. In some twisted way, I was determined to remain miserable until the entire planet cried "Uncle" and acknowledged my right to be miserable. I kept waiting for the Prize Patrol to pull up at my front door, with cameras rolling, and announce to the world, "Ladies and gentlemen, we have searched the world over and here she is: the most miserable person on the planet. Congratulations, Donna Partow!"

The bottom line is: no human being has ever been a perfect parent.

If you've read any of my other books or are even remotely familiar with my ministry, no doubt you know I had a pretty messed-up childhood. I've been writing about it for more than a decade, much to my family's chagrin. I really didn't care whether my stories hurt other people's feelings, because the only people who objected when I turned my childhood trauma into my very own Major Motion Picture were the people who hurt me in the first place. I was the one who'd been wronged, and that gave me full literary license.

But I'm starting to grow up a little bit lately, and I've realized:

Even though your childhood was largely shaped by other people's choices, YOU are the only one who can decide where to go from there.

Will you stay stuck in Major Motion Picture mode forever? Replaying old scenes, rehearsing old hurts? Or will you find a way to move on, by putting your past into perspective? You can't control what happens to you, but you can always choose how you respond. You can't change your childhood, but you can certainly decide what type of adult you want to be. You can sink down or rise above. The choice is yours.

The first problem we need to put into perspective is the universal inadequacy of our parents. They may have been saintly or sickly, but the bottom line is: no human being has ever been a perfect parent. The range of imperfection is admittedly broad: everything from abuse and abandonment to June Cleaver. Since I don't know where your childhood falls on that continuum, I've decided to stick to the middle ground with a biblical example almost anyone can relate to: parents who loved their children but made some pretty serious mistakes anyway. The parents are Isaac and Rebekah, and one of their biggest mistakes was playing favorites.

It happens in almost every home. Nevertheless, parents do untold damage to all of their children when they form an unhealthy attachment to one. Often the purpose is to fashion that child into a miniature version of themselves. Have you ever met someone you knew had a problem, but you just couldn't figure out what it was? You were like, "What is wrong with that woman?" Then you met her mother. Lightbulb moment! The Bible talks about the sins of the father, but let's start with the sins of the mother. Moms pass on many destructive behavior patterns, and we may not even realize we're still carrying them into adulthood until we dig around a bit. So grab a shovel and let's get some dirt to work with.

The greatest Major Motion Picture of all time is, of course, the Bible. And in the beginning, there was favoritism:

> The boys grew up, and Esau became a skillful hunter, a man of the open country, while Jacob was a quiet man, staying among the tents. Isaac, who had a taste for wild game, loved Esau, but Rebekah loved Jacob.
>
> Genesis 25:27–28

Jacob turned into a little mama's boy who stayed in the house cooking all day. Along with cooking lessons, his mother also taught him how to be a deceiver:

> Rebekah said to her son Jacob, "Look, I overheard your father say to your brother Esau, 'Bring me some game and prepare me some tasty food to eat, so that I may give you my blessing in the presence of the LORD before I die.' Now, my son, listen carefully and do what I tell you: Go out to the flock and bring me two choice young goats, so I can prepare some tasty food for your father, just the way he likes it. Then take it to your father to eat, so that he may give you his blessing before he dies."

"Why don't I change? Probably so I can keep on telling my sob story."

125

Jacob said to Rebekah his mother, "But my brother Esau is a hairy man, and I'm a man with smooth skin. What if my father touches me? I would appear to be tricking him and would bring down a curse on myself rather than a blessing."

His mother said to him, "My son, let the curse fall on me. Just do what I say; go and get them for me."

Genesis 27:6–13

Notice Rebekah doesn't miss a beat. She develops this elaborate ruse to trick her husband and manages to pull the whole thing off, even though he suspects something's going on. When Jacob takes the food into the room, his father repeatedly questions him, but he doesn't crack under the pressure. His mother would be proud! In fact, he shoots off four lies in rapid-fire succession:

I am Esau your firstborn (v. 19).

I have done as you told me (v. 19).

Here's my personal favorite: *The LORD your God gave me success* (v. 20). That's classic, isn't it? He's lying to help God along.

Verse 24 brings lie number four. His father asks him point-blank, "Are you really Esau?" Again, without flinching: "*I am*," he replies.

Obviously, this wasn't the first time these two had conspired to pull the wool over Dad's eyes. I'll bet this was common practice. It's common practice in plenty of homes today. "Okay, kids, we're gonna do such and so, but don't tell your dad." Or sometimes it's the old, "Well, we don't want to upset your father, so he doesn't need to know about the phone call from your teacher today." So we're lying to him because we care about him. When you really love someone, you lie to him to protect his feelings, right? Oh, wait, that's deception. Not good. Crazy how we train our kids to deceive, then we wonder why they turn around and deceive us, or their spouses, or the authorities in their lives. These behavior patterns really do have a way of sticking with us.

We catch up with Jacob many years later and guess what? He's still deceiving people:

> Then Laban said to Jacob, "What have you done? You've deceived me, and you've carried off my daughters like captives in war. Why did you run off secretly and deceive me?"

> Genesis 31:26–27

So there's no question that mothers have an incredible impact on the behavior patterns of their children, even when those children are well into adulthood. Here's a question worth answering:

What destructive behavior patterns are you carrying from one of your parents?

Deception isn't the only destructive pattern passed on to Jacob. He also fell into Mom and Dad's trap of favoritism:

> Now Israel [Jacob] loved Joseph more than any of his other sons, because he had been born to him in his old age; and he made a richly ornamented robe for him. When his brothers saw that their father loved him more than any of them, they hated him and could not speak a kind word to him.

> Genesis 37:3–4

It's important to note that Joseph's problems began with his grandparents' decision to play favorites, which

127

was passed to his parents who continued the pattern. Surely you've noticed this in your own family and in the lives of those around you. Traditions, favorite recipes, and inside jokes aren't the only things that get passed from generation to generation. Alcoholism, obesity, incest, and every other human dysfunction do indeed run in families, and will continue forever until someone says, "Enough!" Here's another painful question, but I think it's an important one to address right about now:

What destructive patterns are you passing on to your children?

It just about *kills* me to admit this, but I've managed to pass on *the* most painful and destructive pattern from my childhood: feeling like an outcast, feeling like I was the only person on the planet from a family in trouble, feeling like the little girl no one wanted to play with in the neighborhood. That feeling—and the actions that resulted from it—has nearly destroyed my life. Yet, now I see one of my daughters acting it out in her own life. It tears me up inside.

Some of you may be thinking *Childhood? That's ancient history. Why are we talking about that? None of my problems have anything to do with my childhood. I thought this book was going to talk about my* real *problem: namely, everybody else.*

Can I be honest with you? Just lay it on the line? I'm talking about childhood because I meet a lot of very childish church ladies. God loves them, but they are childish.

I think many of us get trapped in childish behaviors because we never really came face-to-face with the full impact of the childhood messages we received. I promise not to turn this book into a fishing expedition in which we sit around looking for someone to blame. Quite the opposite. However, we must confront our problems before we can put them into perspective and, ultimately, resolve them.

If you were sent *any* message during childhood other than "God loves you unconditionally," you might have some stuff to deal with. Let me give you some examples of what I'm talking about:

- Keeping track of who invited whom, when and where, and making note of who didn't get invited
- Keeping a mental list of people who've offended you
- Competing for attention and approval in social situations
- Trying to "one-up" other people's stories with tales of your own, your spouse's, or children's (or even grandchildren's) accomplishments
- Pushing your children to perform so your family will be perceived as having the winning team
- Forming cliques and alliances at your church or place of employment
- Engaging in gossip, trying to build yourself up by tearing other people down
- Obsessing over your personal appearance and going to great lengths to look younger than you are
- Working yourself to death outdoing other women, that is, if Susie rents a pony for her daughter's birthday party, you rent an elephant

All of these actions and attitudes are childish. Guess where childish behavior comes from? Your childhood. It's been well said, "Deal with your past or your past will deal with you." If you have a tape playing in your head that goes something like this: "I better do this right or

129

else . . . ," you've got a problem to deal with, and the best way to deal with a problem is by putting things into perspective. So here goes:

Or else what?
Or else what?

What is it you are so afraid of? I guess it depends. If your parents were abusive, you're afraid the "or else" will mean more abuse. If they were controlling, "or else" means tighter controls. If they were the perfect parents and you were their perfect little child, "or else" could simply have been a raised eyebrow or the slightest frown of disappointment. I would encourage you to think and pray about your "or else." In all likelihood, it's like the monster under your bed—a figment of your imagination. Yes, there are often consequences to our actions, but they are rarely as cataclysmic as we imagine.

Let's go back to the story of Jacob and Esau to get an idea of what Jacob was so afraid of. In other words, what was his "or else"?

When the messengers returned to Jacob, they said, "We went to your brother Esau, and now he is coming to meet you, and four hundred men are with him."

In great fear and distress Jacob divided the people who were with him into two groups, and the flocks and herds and camels as well. He thought, "If Esau comes and attacks one group, the group that is left may escape."

Then Jacob prayed, "O God of my father Abraham, God of my father Isaac, O LORD, who said to me, 'Go back to your country and your relatives, and I will make you prosper,' I am unworthy of all the kindness and faithfulness you have shown your servant. I had only my staff when I crossed this Jordan, but now I have become two groups. Save me, I pray, from the hand of my brother

Esau, for I am afraid he will come and attack me, and also the mothers with their children."

Genesis 32:6–11

Clearly, Jacob is thinking *I better appease my brother or else . . .* Or else what? Or else his brother will *kill* him. Murder. Mayhem. Melodrama! Now, where did he get that idea? It was an old, old message planted in his heart by his mother—the guilt-ridden Major Motion Picture star herself:

> Esau held a grudge against Jacob because of the blessing his father had given him. He said to himself, "The days of mourning for my father are near; then I will kill my brother Jacob."
>
> When Rebekah was told what her older son Esau had said, she sent for her younger son Jacob and said to him, "Your brother Esau is consoling himself with the thought of killing you. Now then, my son, do what I say: Flee at once to my brother Laban in Haran. Stay with him for a while until your brother's fury subsides. When your brother is no longer angry with you and forgets what you did to him, I'll send word for you to come back from there."

Genesis 27:41–45

Few people in the Bible can swing into that Major Motion Picture mode quite like Rebekah, the original Drama Queen. Personally, I think she way overreacted, as she so often did. She goes into a panic and takes drastic measures, commanding her son to *flee at once!* Far better to have taken a deep breath and put the problem into perspective. Everyone knows when people get angry they fly off the handle and say things they don't really mean. Things like "I want to strangle her." "I could just

131

rip your head off right about now." Or "I'll make him pay for what he's done."

Instead of calming down, Rebekah gets swept away in the melodrama of the moment—and Jacob gets swept away, too, never to see his mother again. But her Major Motion Picture take on the situation haunts Jacob for two decades. Here he is a grown man with two families and a small fortune, and he's still living in terror, sure his brother is going to kill him the first chance he gets.

Does his brother kill him?

No. In fact, it is obvious from Esau's response that Jacob has totally overreacted:

> But Esau ran to meet Jacob and embraced him; he threw his arms around his neck and kissed him. And they wept.
>
> Genesis 33:4

We can also tell Esau spent plenty of time around Jacob's mentor (their mom) and knew what this whole Major Motion Picture production was all about. Don't miss the sense of humor in his remarks:

> Esau asked, "What do you mean by all these droves I met?"
>
> "To find favor in your eyes, my lord," he said.
>
> But Esau said, "I already have plenty, my brother. Keep what you have for yourself."
>
> Genesis 33:8–9

In other words, Esau said, *"Chill out and calm down. You're acting just like Mom!"* Good advice for all of us, I suspect. Jacob was being driven by an old lie: appease your brother or he will kill you. We all have lies planted in our hearts. Each lie is like a button. And every time one of those buttons gets pressed, we jump! The more buttons you have, the more jumping you do. And the more you jump, the more people you bump into, the more people you hurt. And since you're bumping and jumping all the time, you're hurt and exhausted in the process.

To be honest, I had so many buttons in my heart, all you had to say to me was, "Donna, you look pretty today," and I'd get offended. I'd be thinking, *What? You thought I looked ugly yesterday?* Or if someone said, "Donna, hey, you look like you've lost weight," my gut reaction would be *What? You thought I looked fat?* No matter what anyone said, I was ready to take offense. Of course, if you didn't say anything to me, I'd get offended about that, too. There was just no winning with me.

What was my "or else"? What was the lie I was buying into? Twenty-four hours a day, there was a tape playing in my head: "You better convince people to feel sorry for you *or else* no one will ever play with you. You can never be liked or admired for your strengths; the best you can hope for is pity." I got set free in a big way when I heard a preacher say one time, "You can be pitiful or powerful, but you can't be both." (By the way, that's powerful in the best sense of the word, meaning one who has a powerful impact for the kingdom of God.)

I would urge you to prayerfully consider your "or else." Then put your problems into perspective by defusing the lie. Jacob needed to say to himself, "I acted like a real jerk, and my brother had every right to be angry with me. But that was decades ago, so I'm not going to live in fear anymore. I'll ask my brother's forgiveness so I can get on with my life." In my case, I needed to say, "I don't want or need anyone's pity. I have God's power in my life now. I have kingdom work to do. It's time to grow up and move on."

I can't point to chapter and verse, but I honestly think Jacob eventually grew up and got on with it. However, before we leave the problem of childhood pain, I want to briefly turn our attention to Esau. Two of the saddest verses in the Bible concern him:

> Bless me—me, too, my father!
>
> Genesis 27:34

Those were the words Esau cried on his father's deathbed. He wanted his father's blessing, but it was denied him because he had made a very foolish choice when he sold his inheritance to his brother, Jacob, in return for a bowl of soup. He was certainly free to make that choice; he liked that part. He wasn't so happy when the logical consequences of that choice came home to roost. Sounds like some of us.

Reflecting back on Esau's anguish, Hebrews 12:17 explains:

> Afterward, as you know, when he wanted to inherit this blessing, he was rejected. He could bring about no change of mind, though he sought the blessing with tears.

Jacob eventually broke free from his mother's melodrama. But Esau never recovered from losing his father's blessing. The Bible says *he was rejected*, and few things hurt more than rejection. It's time to look at the sins of the father. A Midwestern pastor once shared with me how churches in his community had organized an outreach to the local prison for Mother's Day. They got organizations to donate greeting cards and told the prisoners, "Here, you can select a card for your mom, write her a note, address it, and we'll put on the stamp and mail it to her." The response was overwhelming. Churches were scrambling to come up with enough greeting cards to meet the demand.

They decided to do the same thing again in honor of Father's Day. Not one prisoner showed up. Not one prisoner wanted to send a card to his father. Not one. The most powerful truth in the universe is that we have a loving heavenly Father. Is it any wonder that Satan works overtime, throughout our childhoods, trying to distort our view of what a father is? Do you believe a father is any of these things?

Absent
Abusive
Unreliable
Angry
Stern (Mr. Bible Answer Man)
Demanding
Disapproving
Disappointed
The Law Enforcer

All of these represent a form of rejection. Until we deal with the problem of feeling rejected by our earthly father, we'll have a tough time receiving the unconditional love of our heavenly Father. Remember how I defined *perspective*? "The art of giving due diminution to the strength of light, shade and colors of objects, according to their distances and the quantity of light falling on them, and to the medium through which they are seen." It's time to put the problem of your imperfect father into perspective. It's time to shed the light of God's truth upon your life and put some emotional distance between you and your pain. It's time to see your dad through a new medium: the medium of God's grace. No doubt your father did the best he could with what he

135

had. But he couldn't give you what he didn't have, and he couldn't tell you what he didn't know.

No matter how imperfect your dad was, surely his imperfections pale in the light of God's infinite perfection. Now that you have the greatest Father in the world, isn't it time to let your other dad off the hook? It's like a woman with a brand-new Mercedes, sitting around bemoaning her fate because her old 1976 Honda Civic doesn't run. Who cares? You have what you need. Be grateful and choose to focus on the good. You have the Perfect Father now:

> How great is the love the Father has lavished on us, that we should be called children of God! And that is what we are!
>
> 1 John 3:1

Ever After, a modern-day Cinderella story starring Drew Barrymore, is one of my favorite movies. In the end, after she has married her handsome prince, she says to her wicked stepmother, "After this moment, I shall never think of you again." She says it with such conviction, we believe her. I'd hate to see a sequel in which Drew Barrymore refused to enjoy her new life, preferring instead to rehash the inequalities of her childhood. I sincerely hope she chose to live happily ever after. That's what happiness is, you know: a choice.

Now that you have the greatest Father in the world, isn't it time to let your other dad off the hook?

If your life were ever to be turned into a Major Motion Picture, it would have to be a Cinderella story as well. Your new Father is the

King of Kings, and that makes each and every one of us a princess. Of course, you already know that, but I wonder if you *really* know it? If every woman who knew intellectually that she is a princess truly believed it in her heart, the local church would be a very different place. Our homes and our workplaces would be very different, as well.

You can never kid a kidder. I knew the Bible from Genesis to maps. I even had "good doctrine." But that didn't prevent me from living like an underprivileged child rather than a princess. I chose to believe the lies in my heart rather than believing the truth in God's Word.

Surely you have heard these truths before, but are they *working* for you? Let me put it another way: Are you *out there* enjoying your life, or are you sitting home by the fireplace, covered in soot, feeling sorry for yourself while you wait for the Fairy Godmother to show up and wave a magic wand over your head?

If that's you covered in soot, you picked up this book in the nick of time. I want you to close your eyes and imagine me waving a magic wand over your head. Click your heels together and say:

Fall under the power of the wand.
Fall under the power of the wand.
Fall under the power of the wand.

Wouldn't it be great if it were that simple? Alas, it's only that simple in Major Motion Pictures. In the real world, no one will wave a magic wand over your problems. At some point you've got to make the choice. Whom will you believe? Will you believe the lies your parents may have inadvertently told you? Will you believe the nonsense fed into your head by your siblings or classmates? Will you believe what people say, or will you believe what God's Word says?

Jacob chose to believe what his mother said and ended up acting like a paranoid nut. Are your beliefs making you nutty? Mine were!

You have no idea how hard-fought these truths are. But if I were to tell you, it would sound like a Major Motion Picture, so I'll just leave it to your imagination. But believe me when I tell you, I spent more years than I care to recall covered in soot, waiting for someone to rescue me from my problems. The Fairy Godmother never did show up and wave that magic wand over me. Instead, I found my Ever After in a personal relationship with God. You can do the same. For help with this, turn right now to the Steps to Freedom section at the back of the book.

If You Think Your Marriage Is a Mess, Check This Out

Nowhere is the Porcupine State of Mind more frequently made manifest than in the marriage relationship. The Porcupine Spouse is absolutely right and, therefore, absolutely miserable. The porcupine can make no allowance for the possibility that her mate may have a good point or two in his own defense; all she can see is: "I'm right; he's wrong." As a consequence, the Porcupine Spouse is an emotional wreck and a pain in the neck.

Before I go any further on the subject of marriage, I want to clarify what I'm *not* talking about. I'm not talking about abusive relationships. If your spouse has a serious addiction problem with alcohol, drugs, gambling, pornography, or chronic infidelity, you need to seek professional help. If your spouse is violent toward you or your children, you need to get to a safe place immediately and stay there until you have solid proof that he has truly repented and gotten the professional help he needs. There's certainly no shortage of abusive relationships in America today. The leading cause of death among women ages eighteen through thirty-four is murder by a spouse, ex-spouse, or significant other. Sad to say, but abusive relationships really do make for Major Motion Pictures, or, at the very least, a Lifetime made-for-television special.

In cases of addiction or abuse, you really are *right* and he really is *wrong*. Even so, I would urge you to take a good, hard look at *how* you ended up with an unhealthy partner, because birds of a feather usually flock together. Surely, there is *something* inside you that attracted you to him and vice versa. No doubt there were signs of impending trouble before you married him, but you chose to go full speed ahead anyway. Why? When you perceived danger, why didn't you turn back? Something to think about. When I went through a recovery program for battered women, the teacher often said, "The next abuser is always worse." I'll never forget the day she looked me in the eye and said, "Your next abuser will kill you." Let me tell you, that got me *very* motivated to deal with my "issues."

But it's starting to sound like I'm writing the script for a Major Motion Picture, so let's shift gears in a hurry. Life is rarely simple, and it's rather unusual for one person to be *completely right* while the other is *completely wrong*. Wherever two or more are gathered, there's usually plenty of blame to go around.

With those disclaimers in mind, let's dig into God's Word with a view toward getting a perspective on our marriage problems. We're about to look at a rather depressing example of a chronically disappointing marriage, but if you'll stick with me, I think we can find some hope and healing on the other side. The tale of woe begins in Genesis 29:16, when we meet two sisters:

> Now Laban had two daughters; the name of the older was Leah, and the name of the younger was Rachel. Leah had weak eyes, but Rachel was lovely in form, and beautiful.
>
> Genesis 29:16–17

I believe in the original Hebrew that means Leah had the dreaded pear shape and Rachel had big boobs. When I get to heaven, my first question for God will be, "How come the women who got big boobs *also* got thin thighs? How is that fair?" As for the phrase *weak eyes*, that was probably just a polite way of saying she was hard on the eyes. Anyway, you may recall that a guy named Jacob was madly in love with Rachel, but Rachel's dad pulled a dirty trick on him. Instead of sending Rachel to the wedding ceremony, he sent Leah, covered up in a veil. It must have been a candlelight ceremony, because Jacob apparently got the shock of his life when he woke up the next morning and realized he'd married the wrong sister.

You know what's so sad? Leah's dad actually thought he was doing her a favor. Oh the heartache we cause our children when we try to *help them out*. Jacob pitched a fit about the situation, and his father-in-law offered a compromise:

The Porcupine Spouse is an emotional wreck and a pain in the neck.

> He finished the week with Leah, and then Laban gave him his daughter Rachel to be his wife.
>
> Genesis 29:28

So Leah had exactly *one week* to try to win her husband's affection. It didn't work:

141

> Jacob lay with Rachel also, and he loved Rachel more than Leah.
>
> Genesis 29:30

Obviously, this must have been a heartbreaking situation. Even when Leah finally gets a bit of good news, she still describes her life as miserable:

> When the LORD saw that Leah was not loved, he opened her womb, but Rachel was barren. Leah became pregnant and gave birth to a son. She named him Reuben, for she said, "It is because the LORD has seen my misery. Surely my husband will love me now."
>
> Genesis 29:31–32

So she's in a miserable marriage, but now that she has a baby, everything is going to be great, right? Okay, maybe not. (You'd be surprised how many women have tried this at home.) A year or so later, apparently her husband still doesn't love her, and Leah says God himself has heard all about it. I wonder who told him?

> She conceived again, and when she gave birth to a son she said, "Because the LORD heard that I am not loved, he gave me this one too." So she named him Simeon.
>
> Genesis 29:33

Before long, poor Leah lowers her expectations a little. With Simeon she was asking for her husband to *love* her, but as we shall soon see, she decides to settle for *attachment*. Have you ever felt that way in your marriage? Like you were *settling*? Have you ever thought, *I'm not asking for Love Story or the romance of the century. If only the man would just be a little attached to something other than* _____. You can fill in the blank with whatever your husband is more attached to than you, whether it's his work, his buddies, or his golf game.

But before you drift into Major Motion Picture mode, imagine how much worse you'd feel if your husband was attached to your sister. Not just any sister, but your stick-thin, supermodel sister with the big boobs. I think that's what Leah was up against:

> Again she conceived, and when she gave birth to a son she said, "Now at last my husband will become attached to me, because I have borne him three sons." So he was named Levi.
>
> Genesis 29:34

Before I tell you what I really believe about Leah, I want to give a little credit where credit is due. At least she allows hope to spring eternal in her marriage. She gets pregnant yet again and thinks, *This is going to turn the tide. I'm on the upswing here. I can feel it.* But alas, she's obviously disappointed again. We can assume at least another year went by, probably much longer:

> She conceived again, and when she gave birth to a son she said, "This time I will praise the LORD." So she named him Judah.
>
> Genesis 29:35

Well, Leah has finally gotten it right. Aren't you proud of her? At long last, it appears she has realized that her husband is not going to meet all her needs. I often tell women that when you stop expecting your husband to fulfill you, very often he'll have a change of heart toward you. When you stop clamoring for his attention, he'll actually *want* to pay attention to you.

So Leah is on the right path now. She is praising the Lord. She's at peace. She's been set free from that

Porcupine State of Mind. She's on a spiritual high with Jehovah. Maybe she has been to a ladies retreat or something. I don't know, but she has a new attitude. And as we all know, when you praise the Lord, you open the door for God's blessings. Hallelujah. Praise the Lord. Let the rejoicing begin.

It's so interesting how God works. While I was initially writing this, I heard a preacher deliver a sermon on the life of Leah. Guess what? The pastor stopped right here so the story could end on a high note. The message was simple: Leah did it God's way, the formula worked, and she lived happily ever after. Wow, sounds like Major Motion Picture material to me!

Unfortunately, that's not where the story ends. The Bible isn't simplistic, and it isn't afraid to tell the whole truth. I don't know why we are. So much of what passes for truth in the church these days is just a beautiful portrait of the way life ought to be. Ought to be, but isn't. It ought to be true that if you are a good wife, eventually your husband will get with the program. It ought to be true, but it isn't. Is it?

> The Bible isn't afraid to tell the whole truth. I don't know why we are.

Are you ready for the very next sentence? It's not even the next *verse*! It's the next sentence of the *same verse*:

Then she stopped having children.

Genesis 29:35

Now, in our culture that might be considered a blessing. But not in ancient Hebrew culture. Having children was pretty much the *only* sign a woman had that she was blessed by God. So to stop having children, to Leah, was an incredible disappointment. She had derived her entire identity from her ability to produce children for her husband. It was the sole source of her self-esteem. What went wrong? I mean, the poor woman finally got it right. She was working the magical formula:

Stop expecting your husband to meet all your needs	+	Praise God	=	Whatever particular blessing you're in the market for

Looks like a great formula. What's the problem? God's not into formulas. Because formulas don't work. It ought to be true that if you do A + B, you are guaranteed to get C. But that is not the way the real world works. Life isn't that simple, although we would like to believe it is. And the Bible isn't that simplistic, although you'd never guess that by listening to some Bible teachers today.

One of my former neighbors went through a terrible ordeal when she discovered her husband was having an affair. Her church carefully explained to her the formula for fixing her marriage. She worked the formula with all her might. But guess what? Her husband chose to leave her for this other woman anyway. She was completely devastated. She couldn't change the choices her husband made, no matter how hard she tried. No matter how hard she prayed, his mind was made up. So he filed for divorce and married the infamous other woman.

Some of you know firsthand what I'm talking about. It's time for the church to get a reality check: You can stand in faith for your marriage. You can also stand on your tippy toes. You can stand on your head. Nevertheless, that other person may never change. Leah tried it all, but Jacob never changed his attitude toward her.

I've got a news flash for you. You'll probably hate me for this one: We cannot control other people. Not with formulas. Not even through prayer. We can profoundly influence people through prayer, but we can't control them. Prayer can open up incredible opportunities for a person to turn their life over to God, but God won't force himself on anyone.

God's message to each and every person on the planet is "Choose ye this day." To our husbands, God says, "Choose ye this day." While I'm at it, I might as well mention:

To our children, God says, "Choose ye this day"
To our friends and loved ones, God says, "Choose ye this day"
To total strangers . . .

You get the idea: God won't force himself on anyone. This is where our nice, neat little Christian formulas go haywire, especially where marriage is concerned. Because while you are choosing to be a great wife and mother, your husband is free to make contradictory choices. Then you're left thinking, *I did A + B . . . where's my C?*

You've got all your good points. You're absolutely right. Next thing you know, you're back in that Porcupine State of Mind.

I can't tell you how many Christian women I meet whose husbands (or kids or grandkids or sons-in-law, etc.) are making choices that rock their worlds. It is alarming how many husbands are choosing pornography these days. Yes, Christian husbands. Pornography addiction is literally an epidemic among Christian men, even (some would say *especially*) among pastors. You name it—if it's happening in the world, it's happening to nice Christian people. Anyone who tells you otherwise is either dreaming or trying to sell you something.

My guess is that every woman reading this book has at least one person in her life who has made choices that have broken her heart. And for many of you, that person is your husband. Jacob chose to love Rachel more than Leah. Period. Beginning AND end of story.

I suspect many of you can think of a person you've prayed for, and you've watched God give that person one opportunity after another to change course. To turn around. To have a change of heart. God has done everything but come down before that person and say, "Choose me right now or I'm gonna smack you upside your head." He may even come down and say, "Choose your wife right now or you'll be sorry." But some people just stubbornly refuse to get with the program.

You are right. That person is wrong. How far do you think that will get you?

Back to our Major Motion Picture story: Leah grows increasingly desperate. She tries the old Sarah trick of producing children through her maidservant. I'm not even going into that whole mess, except to say she named one of these sons "How happy I am!"

> You name it—if it's happening in the world, it's happening to nice Christian people.

Leah is happy with herself. Her father failed her by marrying her off to a man who didn't love her. Her husband failed her by choosing to love her sister instead, even though Leah produced more sons for him. She tried working the *formula* and that failed her, so she feels like God has failed her. Of course, God never fails, but don't tell Leah that. That's why she took matters into her own hands. It looked like it was working, so she was happy—at least for a season. Her attitude was: "I'll do it my way. I'll get what I need however I can get it. I don't care who gets used or who gets hurt in the process. The ends justify the means." Ever been there? Her happiness is short-lived, though. We catch up with Leah some time later in a bitter exchange with her sister.

> During wheat harvest, Reuben went out into the fields and found some mandrake plants, which he brought to his mother Leah. Rachel said to Leah, "Please give me some of your son's mandrakes."
>
> Genesis 30:14

Just as an aside, it's important to note that mandrakes were believed to promote fertility and prevent miscarriage, so Rachel was clearly on a mission to get pregnant. Leah had no intentions of helping her sister solidify her position as The Perfect Wife:

> But she said to her, "Wasn't it enough that you took away my husband? Will you take my son's mandrakes too?" "Very well," Rachel said, "he can sleep with you tonight in return for your son's mandrakes."
> So when Jacob came in from the fields that evening, Leah went out to meet him. "You must sleep with me," she said. "I have hired you with my son's mandrakes." So he slept with her that night.
>
> Genesis 30:15–16

How's that for romance? I mean, what does this tell you about the condition of this woman's marriage? She has finally hit rock bottom. She has to buy a night in bed with her own husband. Does that help put your marriage problems into perspective or what? To describe her marriage as a disappointing relationship would be the understatement of the century. Someone needs to begin production on this Major Motion Picture immediately. This is serious melodrama, and that's no exaggeration. What's so frustrating is that Leah is absolutely right. Just think about all the good points she had in her favor. I'll bet her silent sermons went something like this:

Point #1   I am the older sister, and that entitles me to certain rights.

Point #2   I am the first wife, and that entitles me to certain privileges.

Point #3   I gave birth to Jacob's firstborn son, and that entitles me to a place of honor.

Point #4   Besides all of that, Rachel is so superficial, okay? I may be ugly, but I'm deep.

Point #5   After all I've done for you, Jacob, bearing you all these sons and giving you my servant, how can you treat me like this? It's not right. It's not fair.

I can't prove this, but I think Leah lived most of her life in a Porcupine State of Mind. She had a lot of great points, but her husband obviously avoided her like . . . well, like she was a porcupine. You know things are pretty bad when you have to pay just to get your husband to come to your tent for one night.

We're sitting here feeling sorry for Leah, but the fact of the matter is, I just ordered the complete TNT Bible Video Collection, and not one of the movies is entitled *Leah*. There is, however, one entitled *Jacob*. Leah's husband had his share of heartache. Look what his father-in-law put him through, working him fourteen years for two wives. I can't imagine my husband putting up with two wives; he's got all he can handle with one wife.

Imagine if he had me *plus someone like me who couldn't stand me*. That man would never come home from work. I can hear him now, "Hi, honey, just wanted to let you know I'll be working late for the rest of my life."

What was Jacob's perspective on this marriage? He never wanted Leah for a wife in the first place. I'm sure he had resentment of his own. He was tricked into marrying her. And I wouldn't be surprised if she played a part in the game. She could easily have said, "Hey, Jacob, it's me, Leah, here under the veil. My dad's trying to trick you. Danger! Warning!" Since when does Leah keep quiet? We don't know if it was all Laban's idea or not. We've seen enough of her persistence and her personality to guess that maybe in the days leading up to the wedding, she was tormenting him: "Dad, it's not fair. I'm the oldest. I should get married first. How come Rachel always gets her way?" You remember the Porcupine State of Mind and all those good points? Maybe Leah hammered those good points relentlessly into her father's head until he couldn't stand it anymore and came up with this little scheme.

> There's something about a person crying out in desperation that God simply cannot walk away from.

We don't know for sure, of course. But I wouldn't be surprised if Leah had a hand in trying to *trap* Jacob, then resented him for feeling *trapped*. Oh, I know that one hurt! I'll bet there are more than a few of you reading these pages who are only too familiar with that little game and its inevitable results.

You want to know what intrigues me most about this whole situation? We saw that Leah had worked the formula: *If I do A + B, God will be so proud of me, he'll surely give me C.* But God didn't get with the program, did he? However, when Leah hit rock bottom, when she was at the absolute end of herself, stripped of dignity, stripped of hope, done playing games—when she threw up her arms and said, "God, do you see this mess? Please hear me when I cry"—then she had God's attention. Then he gave her the desire of her heart:

> God listened to Leah, and she became pregnant and bore Jacob a fifth son.
>
> Genesis 30:17

Underline that one in your Bible, sisters. God listened to Leah. God listened to her, and he will listen to you. So, does Leah finally get it? Does she finally understand that God isn't working a formula here? Does she finally understand that God wants her heart? That he just cannot resist a broken and contrite heart? There's something about a person crying out in desperation that God simply cannot walk away from. Does Leah finally get it? No, no, a thousand times no. She doesn't get it at all:

> Then Leah said, "God has rewarded me . . . for giving my maidservant to my husband."
>
> Genesis 30:18

I don't know about you, but I want to strangle this woman. She still thinks it's about being *right*! But it's not about being right, and it's not about working the formula. It's about your *heart*. In this chapter, we've followed Leah for I don't know how many years, and she doesn't seem to have learned anything. Nothing.

> Leah conceived again and bore Jacob a sixth son. Then Leah said, "God has presented me with a precious gift.

151

This time my husband will treat me with honor, because I have borne him six sons." So she named him Zebulun.

Genesis 30:19–20

The implication behind the words "this time" is that the man still does not honor her. She has borne him six children, plus given him her maidservant who bore him two sons. And still, Leah is just second-rate to him. Second-rate. Runner-up.

Eventually, the entire clan heads back to Jacob's homeland. On the way, they get word that Jacob's brother, Esau, is coming out to meet them. If you remember the story, you know these brothers didn't part on good terms, and Jacob is afraid that Esau might try to kill him and his family. Frankly, he probably deserves it. So he arranges his family in order of importance—with the most valuable members last, so they will be the least vulnerable to attack:

Jacob looked up and there was Esau, coming with his four hundred men; so he divided the children among Leah, Rachel and the two maidservants. He put the maidservants and their children in front, Leah and her children next, and Rachel and Joseph in the rear.

Genesis 33:1–2

He gives the most protection not to Leah—his first wife, the one who bore him the most children—but to Rachel, because he loved her more. To the bitter end, and I do mean the *bitter* end, Leah lived her life in second place. Always second place.

Do you know what it is to be second place? Second place in your husband's heart? There's someone or something else that's first for him. I meet women who are second place after their mother-in-law. They married a mama's boy. Others are second place after his career. This one's painful: second place after his ministry. Second place after golf or football games. Second place after *the other woman*. Second place after a long line of *other women*. Second place after the entire planet. Anything, everything, and everyone is more important than you, because you are second place in your husband's life.

Jacob was not an evil man. In fact, the Bible clearly demonstrates that he loved God and became a better person as he aged. But he never did change his heart toward Leah. Perhaps your husband is not bad either. Maybe he doesn't cheat on you. He doesn't beat you up. He's not an alcoholic. What right do you have to complain? You haven't got an ounce of Major Motion Picture material to work with. So many women have it much worse than you do. You're just second place. Even your pain is second place. First place goes to women who have real marriage problems. Major Motion Picture–sized problems. They have something specific they can point to: he had an affair. He walked out. They are first in line for sympathy. You? You're second place.

Leah was always second place. So sad. But let me ask you something:

Where was God in the midst of all this?

We have gotten so swept up in Leah's melodrama that we've managed to lose sight of what truly mattered in her life. Let's sift through all the nonsense about her desperately trying to win Jacob's approval and see if we can find God amid the rubble:

The LORD saw that Leah was not loved.

Genesis 29:31 (italics added)

The LORD saw. Those are powerful, perspective-altering words, aren't they? When you realize God sees. He knows the whole truth about your situation. If you want to find hope and healing, if you want to find rest for your weary soul, I encourage you to ponder these two words: *God sees.* In fact, one of God's names is El Roi, the God Who Sees. He's not fooled. He knows exactly who's right and who's wrong. God will take care of it in the end. And the one who is right will be vindicated and given her just reward. As it was said of Jesus, may it be said of us: "When they hurled their insults at him, he did not retaliate; when he suffered, he made no threats. Instead, he entrusted himself to him who judges justly" (1 Peter 2:23).

God listened to Leah.

Genesis 30:17 (italics added)

God listened to Leah, just as God listens to you. Cry out to him. Don't cry out to your friends. What can they possibly do? They can't even change their *own* husbands! Porcupines waste all their time and energy trying to get people to feel sorry for them or offer them advice or rescue them from their mess. That's why they've got to tell all their good points to anyone who gets within a mile of them, which explains why everyone stays a mile away. You have a choice concerning how to handle your problems: you can take them to the phone or you can take them to the Throne. Which will do you more good? God is always listening, so why not talk to him? Try it. It's the ultimate cure for the Porcupine State of Mind and the ideal way to put your problems into perspective.

God *had an eternal plan* for Leah's life.

154

I want to show you something rather intriguing about Leah. Even though she's not mentioned by name, we find out something very significant about her life on the very first page of the New Testament:

> A record of the genealogy of Jesus Christ the son of David, the son of Abraham:
> Abraham was the father of Isaac,
> Isaac the father of Jacob,
> Jacob the father of Judah and his brothers,
> Judah the father . . .

> Matthew 1:1–3

Stop right there. We don't need to go any further. Judah was the son of Leah. Leah was one of the grandmothers of Jesus! God saw and God listened, but more than that, God had a plan. With the birth of Judah, Leah *had fulfilled God's primary purpose for her life.* I didn't say it was her only purpose. Nor am I saying women have no function other than giving birth. But I would like to think that if my grandchild was the Savior of the world, I might cheer up a little bit. My point is: We like to tell ourselves that if God would give us some profound assignment, if only we had a sense of purpose, then our lives wouldn't feel like a giant disappointment.

Leah's focus was too narrow.
Leah wanted to save her dignity.
She wanted to save her marriage.
God wanted to save the WORLD.

Leah thought *if only* she could have a son, she could get past the disappointment of being second place in her husband's life. God gave her six sons and she wasn't

155

content. She had a houseful of children—the very thing she prayed for—but it wasn't enough.

Leah chose to focus her attention on the one thing she couldn't have and declared herself "miserable." No one can deny that this marriage relationship was tough, but she also had many blessings. She was the mother of six of the tribes of Israel and the grandmother of Jesus. Rachel may have had a husband who adored her, but Leah was handpicked by God to be part of Jesus's ancestral line.

Sometimes the pain of a disappointing relationship can be so overwhelming that we let it overshadow all the good things in our lives. Don't let that happen to you. Instead, seek God's perspective on your life. I want to share one final thought before we close this rather long, sad chapter:

- God spoke to Abraham (Gen. 17:9)
- God spoke to Abraham's wife, Sarah (Gen. 18:15)
- God spoke to Isaac (Gen. 26:2)
- God spoke to Isaac's wife, Rebekah (Gen. 25:22–23)
- God spoke to Jacob (Gen. 28:13)
- But apparently God had nothing to say to Jacob's wife, Leah

Are we honestly supposed to believe God wanted to speak to *everyone else* who was part of this great plan of his? Everyone else but Leah? No way! If she would have let go of her Porcupine State of Mind for two minutes, if she would have turned off all that nonsense running through her head day and night, I feel certain God would have let her in on his plan. God loves to share his heart, his eternal perspective. He loves to let his children "in" on what he's up to in the world. But Leah wouldn't listen.

God wants to share his eternal perspective with you. Will you listen? It's time for some of you to let go of being right and start aggressively pursuing the need to be healed. You need to get God's perspective on your marriage. Maybe, just maybe, it's accomplishing far more good than you could ever imagine. Maybe God has blessings in store for you that would astonish you!

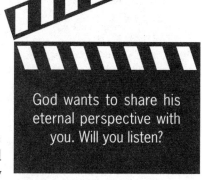

I don't want to be a porcupine here and give you my whole sob story. But I'm telling you straight up: this is one lesson I have learned the hard way. If I were to tell you how

God wants to share his eternal perspective with you. Will you listen?

close to home this story hits for me personally, it would shock your socks off. The only way I have found any hope, any healing, is by turning to God and saying:

I need your perspective.

God, you see me, so tell me what you see.

God, you listen to me, so help me to listen to you.

God, you have a mighty plan for me. Help me to let go of my Porcupine State of Mind long enough to grab hold of your vision and live my life with power and purpose.

If no one else on earth ever acknowledges what has happened to you, how hurt you've been, how profoundly disappointed you have been, please rest assured, God knows. Rest, my sisters. Let your weary heart and soul rest in the knowledge that:

God sees.
God listens.
God has a plan for you.

Listen and let him tell you all about it.

I Never Dreamed Parenting Would Be This Hard

So far, this book has been a breeze to write. It took me two days to get to this chapter . . . then I came to a screeching halt. I have absolutely no clue what to say about parenting other than what I've already stated in the title: I never dreamed parenting would be this hard. The mere thought of writing about it brought me to tears. I hate to rehash the cliché about suddenly discovering just how smart my parents were, but it's a fact. I didn't have my first child until I was almost thirty, so I had plenty of years to sit in judgment upon my own parents before coming face-to-face with the painful truth. And in judgment I sat. They were weighed in the balance and found wanting. I declared them guilty of everything from failing to feed me enough fresh vegetables to being entirely responsible for every mistake my seven siblings and I ever made.

Now I'm the parent. And if I could get my children to eat a fraction of the vegetables—fresh, frozen, canned, or otherwise—I consumed as a child, we could start to make some headway around here. I wake up every morning and pray God will enable me to be "a godly, joyful, effective mother." You can't imagine how many times, when asked for my prayer requests at women's Bible study, the only thing I've asked is that "God would enable me to be a godly, joyful, effective mother." But just to give you an idea, I literally caught one woman rolling her eyes the last time I said it. I know it was the last time, because that incident is why it shall remain the last time.

Recently, a woman told me with great conviction: "You do know that the mother sets the atmosphere of the home, don't you?" Yeah, I've heard it many times, and it always does a sensational job of sending me on a guilt trip. Either I'm the exception to the rule or the rule is totally bogus. When I finally get out of bed in the morning (that part sometimes takes a while), I am the most cheerful person on the planet. I must have short-term memory loss or something, because almost without exception, every day I wake up like Dori in the movie *Finding Nemo*, thinking: *"Keep on swimming! Keep on swimming! What do we do? We swim!"* The truth is, I'm so perky it's annoying.

I sincerely believe—at least for the first five or ten minutes—that *today* is going to be a great day! *Today* I'm going to be a godly, joyful, effective mother. *Today* is the day the tide will turn and my kids will realize what a gem of a mother I am. *Today* they will suddenly be transformed into role models for the nation.

Then my kids get out of bed.

Trust me, perky and cheerful are the last words I would choose to describe the atmosphere that then pervades our home. Does anyone know what I'm talking about? I remember being pregnant with my first child and dreaming about how wonderful parenting would be: how I would one day be crowned "International Mother of the Year." Yes, ma'am, I was going to show the world—especially my parents—how to do the job right. How could I fail? I had been assured that if I really loved God and wanted to do things his way, my baby would sleep eighteen hours a day, while I carefully managed the remaining six hours of her blissful existence. From there, the training would continue as my children quietly learned to cheerfully obey my every word. At least, that's what the *Stepford Parent* screenplay called for.

Unfortunately, the script had to be thrown out the window even before I left the hospital with my new bundle of _____ (well, the right word escapes me). One of the nurses pulled me aside and explained, "We have a name for your daughter." *How delightful*, I thought, as a few ideas sprang to mind: *Child prodigy? Gift from heaven? Angel incarnate?* The nurse continued, "We call her the Leader of the Pack." A pregnant pause in the dialogue ensued as I tried to grasp what she was saying, so she added, "You've got a real handful there."

No worries, though. I had graduated from parenting class with an A+. I had the baby's schedule typed up on the computer and her entire life mapped out in my mind. This was going to be a walk in the park. Yeah, right.

I never dreamed parenting would be this hard.

In a previous book, I shared the heartache I endured when my marriage ended in divorce. I, who had homeschooled my children on the side of an isolated mountain in an attempt to shield them from the world and all the heartache therein. I, who had mastered the art of denial and spent so many years looking the other way that I have a permanent crick in my neck, suddenly found myself plunged into a Towering Inferno of anxiety, fear, anger, and remorse. I wrote about hitting rock bottom on the evening of November 17, 2001, as I watched a meteor shower *without* my daughters by my side, tears streaming down my face as I quietly sang "Somewhere Out There." I commented that sharing a meteor shower with my children seemed like such a small thing to ask of the universe. It's time to print a retraction. It's time to put this parenting trip into perspective.

This morning, our church had a visit from some of the Lost Boys of Sudan. Their journey put my meager suffering into perspective. Even as I was gazing at stars from the deck of my beautiful cedar-sided cabin, feeling sorry for myself because my daughters were playing video games at their father's $300,000 home in Scottsdale (one of the wealthiest suburbs in the richest country on earth), the mothers of these boys were either dead or enslaved somewhere in Northern Sudan. Those few mothers who survived long enough to gaze at stars had no clue where their children might be.

Ah, the power of putting our problems into perspective.

I routinely use words like "heartbroken" and "devastated" to describe the emotional trauma of watching my daughters struggle to fit in at the local Christian school. What words would I use to describe my pain if my daughters lived through a fraction of what the Lost Boys had endured? They were driven from their subsistence farms in Southern Sudan when their fathers (and most of their mothers) were slaughtered before their very eyes, along with every other adult in their village. They hid in the bushes while their sisters were raped and kidnapped to be sold into slavery, where they would be raped and tortured some more.

An estimated twenty-six thousand boys began the thousand-mile trek through the blistering heat of the sub-Saharan desert, heading south to Ethiopian refugee camps. Can you imagine *trying* to get to Ethiopia? Most people are trying to get *out* of Ethiopia. Along the way, thousands died of dehydration and starvation. Wild animals stalked the boys, picking off the weariest each day. After three years in Ethiopia, the boys were driven out *en masse* by government tanks. As they scrambled to escape across the Gilo River, thousands were shot, drowned, or eaten by crocodiles.

Amazingly enough, their suffering didn't even warrant a Major Motion Picture in the world's eyes, although you can order an award-winning documentary, *The Lost Boys of Sudan*, off the Internet. Aid organizations estimate that 2 million Sudanese have been slaughtered and another 4 million displaced by the most violent civil war in modern history. But what really tears my heart out is that we can't seem to find the right school for my teenager. It's been like a war; you can't imagine what we've been through.

Perspective.

It makes me half crazy that I can't get my children to eat right or keep their rooms clean; I lose sight of the fact that at least they have food to eat and beds to sleep in. I'm so disappointed because my children don't want to praise the Lord all day long (like their mother does); but at least they know Who he is and have a five-mile-long list of things *to* praise him for. I've long considered it a serious injustice that I can't take my children to church with me on Sundays, because they are with their father on weekends. But at least they are free to worship God without fear of persecution. I get upset because they don't read their Bibles enough, but at least they *have* Bibles. At least they believe—at least for now—that every word on every page is true.

I'm about ready to tear my hair out because my oldest daughter wants to quit piano lessons and I know that's a *huge* Major Motion Picture–sized mistake. Yet a day is soon coming when my children will begin making serious life choices, many with potentially devastating and far-reaching consequences. Maybe I should chill out about piano and save my emotional energy? Nah.

So many Christian women feel like complete failures as moms. I know because I meet them, and I know because I feel the same way. Recently, I was a guest on James Robison's *Life Today* program. The other guests in the studio that day had just returned from a trip to Angola, where they spent time at one of Life Outreach International's feeding centers. *Many* of the mothers they encountered did not get their children to the feeding center in time, so even though their children were still alive and food was now readily available, their bodies had so completely shut down that they rejected the food. Their babies died in their arms with an abundance of food in the next room. What word do you think these mothers would use to describe themselves?

Now that we've put things into global perspective, perhaps the melodrama unfolding in your home seems a bit more like a mellow drama? But even if your drama is mellow compared to the Sudan, your pain is still real. When your children are making bad choices and you feel like you're at the end of your rope, it helps to know you're not alone. And I don't think you are, even though many Christian books on parenting will make you feel otherwise.

I'm sure there are many excellent Christian parenting books out there, but to be honest, I don't read them. Why? Because every one I have ever read was filled with beautiful truths about the way parenting *ought* to be. But as we all know—and occasionally some of us are even courageous enough to admit—there's a big difference between the way life ought to be and the way it is. When I shared this concept with a group of friends over the Internet, here's what one woman wrote in response:

> Parenting is hard, and the church doesn't do a whole lot to help those who are having struggles with their children. And if we are honest, we know that we all struggle at some point. I remember one family in our former church that seemed to have it all together. He was the chairman of the church board, she was a Sunday school teacher, and their two children were perfect. I remember thinking *I wish I had my life in order like them. Why can't my kids be perfect like hers?*
>
> At the same time, we had a wonderful Christian couple in our church who were going through some real difficulties with their teenage daughter. I remember the "perfect mom" saying things to me about how she just couldn't understand why this couple was having such problems and that the parents must be doing something wrong.
>
> We were having a Ladies' Missionary Meeting one month, and the daughters of this "perfect family" were asked to speak. The oldest daughter began to talk about her high school years and about her rebellion, her drinking, and the fights she had with her mom and dad. My mouth dropped open. I couldn't believe it! They weren't a perfect family after all!!! The mom looked like she wanted to crawl into a hole!
>
> I was angry! If only she had been open with their struggles, she could have helped so many people. I vowed then and there that any struggles God allowed me to go through I would be open about and share

Even if you were the most perfect mother ever to walk the planet, your children would still make foolish choices.

them with others. I believe that we fail one another when we don't pass along what we have learned. Our youngest daughter decided she wanted to date a young man who was unsaved. She knew the rule in our house: no dating unsaved boys. Yet she began to sneak around to see him. My husband and I had two choices: pretend that everything in our home was perfect or take our needs to our brothers and sisters in Christ and ask them to lift her up in prayer. We chose to do the second. I know there were people who looked down on us, who thought we were "bad" parents, but I didn't care. I wanted my daughter to repent and get back on the right track. God was faithful in bringing her back to him.

That's reality right there, folks. It ought to be true that if you love God and faithfully impart that to your children, they are guaranteed to follow in your footsteps. It ought to be true, but it isn't. Are you shocked that I just said that? Well, don't you know someone who obviously loves the Lord, yet has one or more children who don't? It's time for the church to come clean. It's time to stop pretending we believe things that *clearly* aren't true, like "If you train up a child in the way he should go, he is absolutely positively guaranteed to believe everything you've ever taught him, right down to the last drop of your theology and style of worship. He's also guaranteed to live exactly the way you think he should live, which includes producing the correct number of grandchildren with the spouse of your choosing. He'll also keep his hair nicely cut, have a good job, and always send flowers on Mother's Day."

Certainly, you can find a handful of verses in Proverbs to support this position. However, the Scriptures teach not only by precept and promise, but by example:

For everything that was written in the past was written to teach us, so that through endurance and the encouragement of the Scriptures we might have hope.

Romans 15:4

Yes, God preserved the wisdom books of Proverbs and Ecclesiastes, but if you'll take a look at your Bible, it contains far more *stories* than abstract sayings. The book of Proverbs contains helpful principles that are *generally true*. However, the Bible is not a dry textbook; it's our family history. So let's explore our family history for a moment and see if we can get a handle on what the Bible really shows us about parenting.

The first children we encounter are, of course, Adam and Eve. I think we can be quite confident that their Father did a flawless job of training them up in the way they should go. He even spent quality time with them every evening. Yet they still rebelled against his authority; they still made an incredibly foolish choice (Gen. 3:6–7).

Even if you were the most perfect mother ever to walk the planet, your children would still make foolish choices. They would, to one degree or another, rebel against your authority. God created every human being with the power to choose. It's called the human will, and it's what separates us from every other created thing. We learn to exert that will by choosing something *other than* what those around us have chosen for us. If you don't believe me, spend time with a toddler.

The next set of children we encounter are Cain and Abel. Even though they were raised in the same home, by the same parents, they chose two completely different paths. One honored God; the other was a murderer (Gen. 4:3–8). By the time we get to Noah, we see that he *alone* walked with God (Gen. 6:1–9). No doubt he had brothers and sisters, but obviously, they made other choices.

Noah had three sons, one of whom, Ham, disgraced his father by telling tales about Noah's sin rather than covering over the offense as his two brothers chose to do (Gen. 9:18–28).

Next we encounter Abram and his two brothers, Nahor and Haran (Gen. 11:27). After Haran died, Abram and Nahor headed out with their father toward the land of Canaan, the Promised Land. But Abram is the one who moves forward with God (Gen. 12:1). Next, there are Isaac and Ishmael (Gen. 16:15 and Gen. 21:2–4). Although God extended his blessing to both sons, it was Isaac who "prayed to the LORD" (Gen. 25:21) and walked in the power of the promise.

Next we encounter Jacob and Esau, not just brothers but *twins*. Yet "Esau despised his birthright" (Gen. 25:34), while Jacob was blessed because he "struggled with God and with men" and overcame (Gen. 32:28). Jacob had twelve sons. Ten conspired to sell one, Joseph, into slavery (Gen. 37:26–29). Joseph is among the godliest men in Scripture, yet we hear virtually nothing of his children, Manasseh and Ephraim.

All of that is just from the first book of the Bible. The pattern continues. Of the approximately 2 million children of Israel, only two were considered faithful enough to enter the land of promise:

> Because they have not followed me wholeheartedly, not one of the men twenty years old or more who came up out of Egypt will see the land I promised on oath to Abraham, Isaac and Jacob—not one except Caleb son of Jephunneh the Kenizzite and Joshua son of Nun, for they followed the LORD wholeheartedly.
>
> Numbers 32:11–12

I can't help wondering what became of Caleb's and Joshua's siblings. Samuel was raised in the same household as Hophni and Phinehas, by the same man: Eli the priest. The Bible tells us plainly, "Eli's sons were wicked men; they had no regard for the LORD" (1 Sam. 2:12). Meanwhile, in a bedroom down the hallway, Samuel heard the voice of God calling and "grew up in the presence of the LORD" (1 Sam. 2:21). So the sons of Eli the priest chose the path of wickedness, while Samuel did not. Nor did Gideon, whose father was a priest of the vile pagan god Baal (Judg. 6:25). Gideon became "a mighty warrior" for the Lord (Judg. 6:12).

David was a man after God's own heart, but his brothers were among those cowering in faithless fear in the face of Goliath and the Philistine army. In fact, his oldest brother "burned with anger at him" and accused him of being "conceited" and "wicked" (1 Sam. 17:28) when David suggested they should take a stand for God.

Can someone please tell me how Saul, one of the creepiest guys in the Old Testament, produced a son like Jonathan? (See 1 Sam. 20:4–17.) Sometimes I swear the worst parents have the sweetest children! Have you ever noticed how well-behaved many children of drug addicts and alcoholics are? How responsible, resourceful, hard working, and obedient they become? It's enough to make me pour myself a drink (just kidding).

And David's kids! Oh, my, now it *really* gets ugly. David, who loved the Lord so passionately and penned all those beautiful psalms. David, who devoted his life to serving the Lord, raised the worst bunch of kids you could ever meet. (Well, there *was* that whole Bathsheba-Uriah mishap.) Let's see if your kids are this bad:

Amnon raped his sister Tamar (2 Sam. 13:1–14)
So Absalom murdered his brother Amnon (2 Sam. 13:23–35)

Next Absalom usurped his father's throne (2 Sam. 15:1–12) and David fled for his life because his own son was out to kill him (2 Sam. 15:13–15)

After Absalom was put to death, his brother Adonijah "put himself forward" and declared "I will be king" (1 Kings 1:5). Instead, Solomon became king. We could talk about how Solomon's sons started a civil war that destroyed the nation of Israel, but I think you've gotten the idea by now. By the way, Solomon is the one who wrote that bit about "they will not depart from it," but his kids sure departed, didn't they? Come to think of it, not only did his kids depart, *he* departed even though he had David for a father.

People make their own choices. Are your children people? Let's merge those two sentences: Your children make their own choices. Whenever I'm speaking, I often tell the story of Esau in detail because there is *so much* we can learn from his life. But the most important lesson for the purpose of this chapter is simply this: Esau's father loved God. Esau's brother loved God. Esau couldn't have cared less. There is *no guarantee* that your children will have a passion for God just because you do. Esau walked away, while his brother Jacob followed God wholeheartedly. All you can do is give your children the opportunity to know God—it's up to them what they choose to do with that knowledge.

After twenty-four years hanging out with Christians, here's my firm conviction: for every Christian mother who says, "*See*, we trained our kids up in the way they should go and they didn't depart from it," there is another Christian parent scratching her head, saying, "*Gee*, we trained our kids up in the way they should go and they *did* depart from it." The first mother can congratulate

170

herself; the second mother doesn't need to waste time condemning herself, because that's what the church is there for. (More on that in the next chapter.) I may be wrong, but I think the *whole counsel of God* (as opposed to isolated snippets) is on my side: some people choose to love and obey the Lord; some people turn their backs and walk away. Your children are people. Some will obey; some will walk away.

I'm not sure if that's depressing or comforting, but I'm pretty sure it's true. C. S. Lewis observed, "God has no grandchildren." Each one of us has to make a personal choice to yield to Jesus.

Before I leave you wondering if parenting is worth the effort, I want to look at this from yet another perspective. It is vitally important for us to find the balance between owning the responsibility to do the best we can with our children and taking on the burden of blaming ourselves for their choices. Up until now, I've focused on lifting the burden of blame. Now I'd like to turn my attention to the other half of the equation: owning our responsibility to do our best. I've been telling you family histories from the Bible; I'd like to tell you some family histories I have learned about firsthand.

As the American Civil War (or War between the States) was drawing to a close, the Confederate army moved from town to town, warning people to make way for the advancing Union army. One day they happened upon a small Virginia farmhouse and told the family they had to leave. But the woman explained, "I am a widow with three small children still at home. I have nowhere else to go." The soldiers tried to convince her to leave. "There is an army coming against you. Don't you understand?" "This is my home," she said. "I believe God has promised to protect us. This is where we'll stay."

171

That night the Union army did sweep through Virginia. And they burned and pillaged everything in their path. The next morning, in the midst of the rubble and the ashes, only one house stood. It was the house of that widow.

Curious, the Confederate soldiers returned to ask, "Who were all those men guarding your house last night?"

Well, we know who they were. God himself sent an army of angels. God asked her to stand firm, and the minute she took a step of faith, he sent down help from heaven to enable her to stand firm. I believe God wants to do the very same thing for every woman who will demonstrate the same faith and determination to stand firm in her own home today.

The true story of that widow's incredible faith has been passed down as a spiritual inheritance, now to the seventh generation of her descendants. Those descendants include my dear friend Joy Morse. In reflecting upon the blessings of God toward her family, Joy recently told me that she does not have a single blood relative who doesn't know the Lord in a personal way. There doesn't appear to be an Esau in the bunch. This family has managed to pass down, generation after generation, a valuable spiritual inheritance. That's not easy to do.

> If you are a First Generation Christian, don't be surprised that fighting to protect your family's spiritual inheritance is a much tougher assignment for you than for the person next to you.

So often the power of faith, the vibrancy, is lost with each passing generation. But that doesn't appear to have happened to them. Not that her whole family is perfect, not that they haven't faced their share of hard times and heartache. They certainly have. But they know whom they have believed and are persuaded that he is able to keep that which they've committed to him against that day (see 2 Tim. 1:12). I know how hard it is to maintain an eternal perspective on parenting. One thing many women struggle with in the midst of all the small stuff that constitutes our daily lives is feeling insignificant. Feeling like we don't have some Major Motion Picture–sized assignment from God. I sincerely hope this family history lesson has helped give you a broader perspective for what's at stake.

The First Generation Christian Fight

May I share some of my family history with you?

I, too, know what it is to wage a mighty battle for my children. I remember one day when I was weary from the fight, I sat down at my kitchen table and just started weeping. My children came over, put their arms around me, and prayed for God to "help Mommy." Mommy clearly needed all the help she could get. When they had finished praying, Leah, then just ten years old, looked at me and said: "Mommy, I think I know why all this is happening to you." "Really, Leah?" I replied. "Tell me about it." And she said, "Mom, I think it's because you are a First Generation Christian."

I was blown away. I asked, "What do you mean by that, Leah?" She said, "Think about it, Mom. No one in your family has ever been a Christian before. You're the only one. Satan knows if he can beat you, it will be easy to steal us kids, then what chance will our family ever have? You have to stand firm, Mom. Don't let him beat you."

My ten-year-old had grabbed hold of a truth that eludes most adult Christians. Scripture plainly tells us, "Your enemy the devil prowls around like a roaring lion looking for someone to devour" (1 Peter 5:8). Lions always target the most vulnerable animal in the pack, and that's usually the youngest. If you are a First Generation Christian, don't be surprised that fighting to protect your family's spiritual inheritance is a much tougher assignment for you than for the person next to you, whose mother and grandmother and great-grandmother were Christians. You are a primary target for attack, not them. It's not your imagination. Your life, and especially your job as a parent, is much more difficult.

I used to look around my church at different women who had been raised in Christian homes, whose families have been Christians for generations, and think: *Her life doesn't look like mine! Why doesn't my life look like hers? She makes it look so easy, and I'm having a nervous breakdown. What is the problem?*

Listen, Satan has limited resources. He has to be strategic in how he deploys his forces. He is not going to waste ammunition on a woman with an unshakable foundation. That's not to say women raised in Christian homes never endure any trials. Of course they do. But the devil knows if he launches an attack against them, he's probably wasting his efforts. What's she going to do? Count it all joy? I mean, where's the fun in attacking that? She's going to call on her extended family, and they'll gather around to support her. Even in the midst of the most painful tragedy, she'll stand firm. And the worst part—from the devil's perspective—is she'll end up doing more damage to his cause because people around her will marvel at her faith. I mean, at some point, he just sees he can't beat her. So why bother? She's going to resist the devil, and he's going to flee.

And guess where he'll flee to? Right on over to your house, if you are, in fact, a First Generation Christian. He knows you have no foundation to build on. No support structure. No established supply lines. I mean, before your feet hit the floor in the morning, he's on your case. It's not your imagination. You are not having a nervous breakdown. It is for real. He wants to take you and your family down. He doesn't want your children to inherit a blessing; he wants to destroy them.

And do you know why? Because the devil is a mathematician. He understands about exponential growth. He understands the multiplied impact, generation after generation, of one woman who fights to pass on a spiritual inheritance to her children. Some of you reading this right now are First Generation Christians. I pray that God will give you a vision, right now, of a mighty army coming behind you into the kingdom of God. I pray that you will grab hold of all that's at stake here.

If you are a First Generation Christian—and I'm not talking about attending church; I mean if you are the first person in your family to take seriously the importance of following God, of having a personal relationship with the living God—this message is for you. I believe a lightbulb has just gone on over your head. Maybe now, for the first time in your life, you finally understand why your journey has been so difficult. But I hope you also know, as you've never known before, that it's worth the price. That what you're doing in your life, right now, will make a difference for all eternity. You are fighting the good fight so that your children, and grandchildren, and great-grandchildren might inherit a spiritual blessing. So put your parenting problems into perspective. Is it worth fighting the battle?

Where Are the Musk Oxen?

Now I want to turn my attention to the rest of you. Those of you raised in Christian homes. Sometimes people will come up to me and apologize for not having a testimony. I tell them "testimony" is just a polite way of saying "Boy, you've made a mess of your life." Don't you think it's interesting that if that widow's story had not been passed down, no doubt her descendants would be standing around apologizing for their lack of a testimony? The simple fact is, no family moves from the kingdom of darkness into the kingdom of his blessed light without someone, somewhere, saying, "This is the most valuable possession I have. I'm going to make sure it gets passed down to my children in a way that protects its value." Maybe your mother, grandmother, or great-grandmother paid that price for you, and you just don't know about it.

Don't ever apologize for receiving the greatest gift any parent can give her children: the gift of a spiritual inheritance. But don't squander it either. Don't be like Esau, who saw no value in what his father wanted to pass onto him.

Where are those who will stand in prayer, forming a circle of spiritual protection around the weak? . . . *Where are the Musk Oxen?*

There is no greater gift you can give your children than a godly inheritance. We spoke a few moments ago about roaring lions and how they prey upon the young. I want to shift gears from roaring lions to howling wolves. Up in the Arctic Circle there lives a mighty animal known as the musk ox. When the wolves, which prey upon the young musk oxen, begin to howl, the adult musk oxen form a circle around their young. They stand there, and by the sheer force of their countenance they say to those wolves, "If you want to destroy one of these babies, you'll have to GET PAST ME!" This is extremely rare in the animal kingdom. In fact, there is only one other creature on the planet—the African counterpart of the musk ox—that forms a defensive circle. All other species turn and run in the face of danger.

When I look at the church in America today, I have no choice but to conclude that the wolves are devouring at will. When I hear that the divorce rate in the church is either equal to or higher than the divorce rate outside the church, I know the wolves are devouring at will. When I hear that the teen pregnancy rate is higher among teens raised in evangelical Christian homes than it is in the world at large, when I travel this country listening to tales that just rip my heart out, I know the wolves are on the loose in the church.

And when I look at this situation, one burning question comes to my mind: *Where are the Musk Oxen?* Where are the guardians of the church? Where are the women who have been blessed with a rich spiritual inheritance, the women with all the great kids and the bragging rights? Where are the women who should be mighty in the land? *Where are the Musk Oxen?* Where are those who will stand in prayer, forming a circle of spiritual protection around the weak? Where are those who will stand in the face of the devil and say, "If you want to destroy one more family in this church, you're gonna have to GET PAST ME!" *Where are the Musk Oxen?*

I think one of the greatest tragedies in the church today occurs when those who should be what I call Mighty Musk Ox Warrior Princesses see those who are floundering and struggling in their role as parents—and rather than protecting them, they condemn them. They heap guilt on their heads. They reach in and throw them to the wolves. They judge and condemn.

Let me ask you something. Are there certain women in your church who week after week have the same prayer requests? They never seem to make any serious progress in their spiritual growth. They are embroiled in one mess after another. They seem to be living in a sea of turmoil and chaos. And you smile politely, but inside you are *rolling your eyes*, thinking, "Why can't she just raise her kids God's way? Why can't she just get them with the program?"

Remember the woman in my weekly Bible study I caught rolling her eyes at me?

You can take it to the bank: nine times out of ten, the women who struggle most in the area of parenting—and every other area, for that matter—are First Generation Christians. You know why she can't get it together? Because she didn't have what you had. She didn't have a praying mother. She didn't have a grandmother, sitting in a rocking chair hour after hour, praying for her. Do you believe in the power of a praying grandmother? Then why are you astonished that her life doesn't look like yours? You should be astonished if it does!

Here's what I'm proposing: I want you to invest a portion of your inheritance into the lives of First Generation Christians. A vital part of your spiritual inheritance is the right to approach the throne of grace and intercede for others. It's not enough for you to sit around congratulating yourself, "See, I trained them up right, and they didn't depart from it." Stop being so conceited and selfish! Instead, you need to join the growing army of mighty prayer warriors who choose to surround those struggling families to empower them to create what you have been so freely given: a godly legacy.

When I do this at private church retreats, right about now the Musk Oxen start crying. They realize the women

178

who stood just moments ago—identifying themselves as First Generation Christians—are the very women they've been rolling their eyes at. Next time, stop asking yourself, "What is wrong with that woman? Why can't she just raise her children in the nurture and admonition of the Lord? Why can't she just train them up in the way they should go? Look, her kids are departing! She must have done something seriously wrong!" Instead, go ask her, "Are you, by any chance, a First Generation Christian? Are you the first person in your family to try to be a godly mother?" Then promise to stand in the gap on her behalf.

You have been given a great gift, my sisters—don't you dare apologize for that. But it comes with a high responsibility. And I want to challenge you, with all that is within me, to rise to the occasion. On behalf of First Generation Christians everywhere, I'm begging you: rise to the occasion. We need you. Because we never dreamed parenting could be so hard.

The psalmist wrote, "Though an army besiege me, my heart will not fear; though war break out against me, even then will I be confident" (Ps. 27:3). I'm not trying to make a Major Motion Picture out of a miniseries here. There really is a war being waged for our families. The eternal destiny of many generations to come is at stake. The writer of Hebrews declared, "We are not of those who shrink back and are destroyed, but of those who believe and are saved" (Heb. 10:39). May it be said of you that you did not shrink back, not even in the face of overwhelming obstacles, but that you chose to continue believing God.

Perhaps you never dreamed parenting would be this hard, but let's put things into an even larger perspective: isn't it worth fighting the battle when you realize your children's spiritual inheritance is at stake?

My Church Hurt My Feelings

Last night, I didn't get to sleep at all.

It wasn't indigestion. Not even insomnia. I tossed and turned all night because my church hurt my feelings. And even though I am literally writing the book on the importance of chilling out, I was red-hot with hurt and indignation. Yes, it's true. The very same woman who recently crafted that beautiful treatise on escaping the Porcupine State of Mind (see chapter 1) spent thirty-two solid hours (hence the need to forgo sleep) fuming. Because I know I'm absolutely right and they are absolutely wrong.

I previously stated that nowhere is the Porcupine State of Mind more often made manifest than in the marriage relationship. Based on my experience and informal research, church comes in a very close second. For me personally, it comes in first. My husband and I are both very quick to admit when we are wrong, and it's pretty hard to fight passionately for all your good points in the face of someone who is nodding his head in agreement. Now, if only I could get everyone in my congregation to agree with me when I'm pointing out how wrong they are, my stay on planet Earth would be exponentially more enjoyable.

I don't know about you, but deep inside, one of the main reasons I go to church is to recapture the joyous experience of standing around campfires singing "Kumbaya, My Lord." I became a Christian at a retreat center, and I honest-to-goodness believed I would always feel that joy—not just about God, but about my dear brothers and sisters in Christ. The ones who were holding hands, crying tears of repentance, offering hugs of comfort, and praying for the power of God to be displayed in our midst. The ones who showed me, for the first time in my life, what unconditional love looked like. That's what I thought church was all about.

Man's inhumanity to man is nothing compared to the church lady's inhumanity to other church ladies!

Are you laughing at me and my infinite naiveté?

Or are you plotting to set me straight? Before you write me an email pointing out how wrong I am and how we should go to church to worship God and go for what we can give rather than what we can get, let me save you the trouble. (See how good I am to you? Now you'll have time today for your devotions after all!) I already know that stuff. In fact, I'm one of America's foremost leading experts on what people "should" do and how people "ought" to feel. Not just about church, but about every aspect of human existence. I mean, aren't we all? Don't we all know how life should be and how people—especially other people—ought to behave? I'm not talking about oughts and shoulds here, friend. I'm talking reality. So let's get real and forget the campfire songs. Sometimes going to church feels a lot more like walking into a firestorm of controversy and heated emotions. Few topics have generated more intense reaction on my various Internet support groups than the issue of "Guess What My Church Has Done to Me." Man's inhumanity to man is nothing compared to the church lady's inhumanity to other church ladies! Although apparently a lot of men—especially pastors—are mean to church ladies, too. Well, at least according to the church ladies.

I've certainly had my share of "mean pastors." Let's see: first there was the one who didn't want to perform my wedding ceremony to the man raised in a Muslim country, with whom I ended up spending eighteen of the most difficult years of my life. Maybe that pastor wasn't as mean as a certain someone led me to believe? Then there was the pastor who suggested I "dial it down a notch" just because I was an absolute lunatic. Who could have predicted I would eventually leave that church, friendless and full of regrets? Oh, yeah, he did. Worst of all was the pastor who didn't find me a credible source for information, just because I was a broken and battered remnant of humanity, hanging onto sanity by a thread.

No doubt about it, pulpits are just brimming with mean men.

I'm not alone in this observation. I knew a woman whose pastor had the nerve to suggest that, if she wanted to assume a leadership position in the church (which she did), she should take better care of herself (which she didn't). Is that outlandish or what? Who has time to take a shower, brush her teeth, and put on deodorant when she is eager to be about the Lord's business?

Then there was the woman who wrote to tell me she, too, had been blocked from the ministry God had called her to fulfill. She was ready, willing, and able to teach Bible study at her church. She certainly seemed knowledgeable to me. Who was standing in the way? You guessed it. Another mean pastor. I was convinced she was absolutely right and he was clearly wrong. Then I met her in person and within the first five minutes, the Lord gave me a remarkable revelation: maybe her pastor had a little more sense than I had given him credit for.

Maybe pastors aren't half so mean as their congregations imagine. And something tells me their job is a whole lot tougher than most of us think, in view of the fact that fifteen hundred men leave the pastorate in America *every month* (www.pastorsinpain.com). Maybe that's why the Bible admonishes us to:

> Obey your leaders and submit to their authority. They keep watch over you as men who must give an account. Obey them so that their work will be a joy, not a burden, for that would be of no advantage to you.
>
> Hebrews 13:17

In recent weeks, I've spent hours contemplating many of the "Guess What My Church Has Done to Me" tales I've heard over the years. They seem to fall into two distinct categories: (1) The Real McCoy and (2) My Church Hurt My Feelings. Let me address each in turn.

The Real McCoy

The most obvious example of The Real McCoy that springs to mind is the scandal that rocked the Catholic Church in the late 1990s, when it was publicly revealed

184

that the church had actively covered up countless instances of sexual abuse by priests. Make no mistake about it, though. The Catholics do not have a corner on sexual abuse. I'm quite certain we could uncover just as much evil lurking in other denominations. Do you honestly think the enemy says, "Oh, that's a church. Better not bother anybody in there"? Are you kidding! That's exactly why the forces of evil work overtime wreaking havoc in churches—to embitter people, thereby preventing them from ever becoming productive members of the body of Christ.

I've heard stories that haunt me at night. Tales of children molested in Sunday school. Teenagers seduced by youth ministers or raped by workers at church camp. However tragic these events were, the real tragedy is *not* that the enemy came to steal, kill, and destroy. That's his job description. The real tragedy is when Christians allow his scheme to pay off—when we give in to that "root of bitterness" (Heb. 12:15) and blame the whole church for the actions of a few. It's throwing out the proverbial baby with the bathwater.

While addressing grievous sins committed in the Corinthian church, Paul first insisted upon church discipline:

> But now I am writing you that you must not associate with anyone who calls himself a brother but is sexually immoral or greedy, an idolater or a slanderer, a drunkard or a swindler. With such a man do not even eat.
>
> What business is it of mine to judge those outside the church? Are you not to judge those inside? God will judge those outside. "Expel the wicked man from among you."
>
> 1 Corinthians 5:11–13

He then went on to point out the danger of our sinful response to the sin of others within the context of the body of Christ:

> If you forgive anyone, I also forgive him. And what I have forgiven—if there was anything to forgive—I have forgiven in the sight of Christ for your sake, in order that Satan might not outwit us. For we are not unaware of his schemes.
>
> 2 Corinthians 2:10–11

Paul advocated a balance between holding people accountable for their actions *and* being willing to extend grace so the devil can't keep us trapped in a pit of unforgiveness. Unfortunately, the church today is out of balance. We refuse to hold people accountable. Then, because the offenders are not punished, the wronged individuals try to inflict punishment by withholding forgiveness. It doesn't work.

One of the most significant areas where the church is refusing to exercise accountability is in the area of abusive men. And I think this problem also constitutes The Real McCoy. Controlling, authoritarian men are often drawn to church in the hopes that they can hide their cruel nature under the guise of "wives, submit to your husbands" and "children, obey your parents." Such men appear religious, but they are actually cowards at heart. They are nothing but scared little boys who feel beaten down by the world. Like the man who comes home from work and kicks the dog, these men are looking for someone to kick and a safe place to do it. Sadly, the church too often looks the other way while abusive men lord it over their wives and children.

The final area I would consider The Real McCoy is the whole issue of money. No doubt about it, some churches and ministries are in the highway robbery business. Bible-thumping hucksters have long been the subject of Major Motion Pictures. From *Elmer Gantry* to *Leap of Faith* and *The Apostle*.

Unfortunately, an honest Christian working hard for the Lord is not usually considered the right stuff for a Major Motion Picture . . . or the evening news for that matter. Instead, the focus is on the creeps and crooks among us. However unfair that may seem, until we as the body of Christ take action to stop these people, the church as a whole must sport a black eye. We are one body, remember?

> There should be no division in the body, but . . . its parts should have equal concern for each other. If one part suffers, every part suffers with it; if one part is honored, every part rejoices with it.
>
> Now you are the body of Christ, and each one of you is a part of it.
>
> 1 Corinthians 12:25–27

Church charlatans prey upon the weak, the lonely, the elderly, the down-and-out, and the desperate. Not everyone has had the same education and opportunity in this world. As a result, some people are more vulnerable than others. Whether a person is desperate for a physical or financial miracle, a miracle in their marriage, or even a weight-loss miracle, hucksters can sniff them out and know how to exploit their vulnerabilities.

This is nothing new, of course. In 2 Corinthians 2:17, Paul writes, "Unlike so many, we do not peddle the word of God for profit." Unlike so many! There you have it. The Bible tells us right up front: there really are people who use Christianity as a way to make money. I won't even go into the countless stories of

187

the pastor running off with the building fund cash. No doubt every town in America has had such a scandal at one point or another. Paul repeatedly pointed out that many people were preaching the gospel for wrong motives:

> It is true that some preach Christ out of envy and rivalry, but others out of goodwill. The latter do so in love, knowing that I am put here for the defense of the gospel. The former preach Christ out of selfish ambition, not sincerely, supposing that they can stir up trouble for me while I am in chains. But what does it matter? The important thing is that in every way, whether from false motives or true, Christ is preached.
>
> Philippians 1:15–18

In the following passage, Paul is painting a contrast between his own ministry and others who are preaching in Thessalonica:

> For the appeal we make does not spring from error or impure motives, nor are we trying to trick you. On the contrary, we speak as men approved by God to be entrusted with the gospel. We are not trying to please men but God, who tests our hearts. You know we never used flattery, nor did we put on a mask to cover up greed—God is our witness.
>
> 1 Thessalonians 2:3–5

The clear implication of the phrase "on the contrary" is that others *were* operating from impure motives and *were* trying to trick people. They *were* using flattery to cover up greed. These problems have existed since the dawn of time. As Solomon said, "There is nothing new under the sun" (Eccles. 1:9).

That's why the Bible tells us exactly what we should do when faced with The Real McCoy. We're not supposed to run away or look the other way. It's our responsibility to lovingly confront those who are in the wrong:

> If your brother sins against you, go and show him his fault, just between the two of you. If he listens to you, you have won your brother over. But if he will not listen, take one or two others along, so that "every matter may be established by the testimony of two or three witnesses." If he refuses to listen to them, tell it to the church; and if he refuses to listen even to the church, treat him as you would a pagan or a tax collector.
>
> Matthew 18:15–17

How would you treat a pagan or a tax collector? Hopefully, you would treat them as someone who needs to experience the grace and mercy of God. You wouldn't turn your back on them, but neither would you entrust them with a position of leadership in the church. You wouldn't let them pass themselves off as a Christian. We need to be "wise as serpents and harmless as doves" (Matt. 10:16 NKJV).

So many people seem disillusioned with the church these days. Many of them are sitting in church brokenhearted. But I meet many people in my travels—cab drivers, waitresses, flight attendants, fellow airline passengers, or hotel guests—who tell me (and I hear this all the time), "I'm a Christian, but I never go to church. They're all a bunch of hypocrites!" Then they proceed to tell me their very own "Guess What My Church Did to Me" story. Some of their stories are harrowing; most of them are downright trivial.

Which brings me to the next category: My Church Hurt My Feelings.

189

My Church Hurt My Feelings

Can I just lay it on the line here? I meet a lot of messed-up church ladies (not to mention messed-up ladies who've dropped out of church). They are incredibly insecure and feel terrible about themselves, so they do one of two things and sometimes both. First, they desperately strive to earn approval. And second, they seek to make themselves look better by tearing someone else down. These two activities explain much of dysfunctional church behavior.

Let's say Joan wants to be the new Sunday school superintendent. If she's passed over, she'll either stew or storm out. Then, everyone who gets within earshot will get an earful of Major Motion Picture-isms and "Guess What My Church Did to Me" tales. But let's not imagine such a dreadful outcome. Let's say Joan gets tapped for the assignment. Even supposing God has gifted her to superintend, the undertaking will still result in discord if she is driven by a desire for approval. That's because the desperate yearning for approval is just like any other addiction: insatiable.

Even if the pastor publicly applauds her on five consecutive Sundays, she'll fixate on the one Sunday when Kathy was mentioned instead. It won't matter if nine out of ten Sunday school teachers think she's the best thing since the creation of flannel board; the one person withholding adulation will become the constant topic of her thoughts and, in all probability, her conversations as well. In short, she's an approval junkie. If she doesn't get her fix, God help her family and friends. That's why Paul spells this one out plainly:

Am I now trying to win the approval of men, or of God? Or am I trying to please men? If I were still trying to please men, I would not be a servant of Christ.

Galatians 1:10

190

If you are addicted to approval, do the church a favor and seek it in the world. Otherwise, you'll do more harm than good to the cause of Christ. When you are prepared to live your life before an audience of one, then and only then are you ready to step into a place of ministry:

> I care very little if I am judged by you or by any human court; indeed, I do not even judge myself. My conscience is clear, but that does not make me innocent. It is the Lord who judges me. Therefore judge nothing before the appointed time; wait till the Lord comes. He will bring to light what is hidden in darkness and will expose the motives of men's hearts. At that time each will receive his praise from God.
>
> 1 Corinthians 4:3–5

If you want to avoid falling into the "Guess What My Church Did to Me" trap, ask yourself the following questions before volunteering to serve:

- Can I serve while caring very little if I am judged by others?
- Can I live at peace, based on my own conscience?
- Can I wait patiently for that day when God exposes people's motives—including mine?
- Am I willing to work, not for the praise of men, but for praise from God?

A woman who thinks she can serve both God and man is deceived. When there's not enough approval to feed upon—and for a junkie, there never is—guess what she'll eat? Other people. It's what I call emotional cannibalism (for more on this subject, see my previous book, *This Isn't the Life I Signed Up For*). A cannibal is

191

someone who eats other people. But they don't do it for the taste. They do it because they believe the act of consuming another human being will somehow make them more powerful.

An emotional cannibal is someone who thinks the only way she can lift herself up is by tearing someone else down. If you're looking for modern-day cannibalism, look no further than the First Christian Church in Anytown, USA. It goes something like this: Let's imagine that Teresa and Madeline go out to lunch to talk about plans for the upcoming ladies' retreat. Now unbeknownst to Madeline, Teresa is secretly a cannibal, and poor unsuspecting Madeline has no idea that *she is on the menu.* Sometime between the minestrone soup and the chicken Caesar salad, Teresa turns to Madeline and says, "I really hope you're not planning to sing again this year. Your solo last year really fell flat. I'm thinking my daughter could do something more contemporary." Teresa spends the remainder of the luncheon bragging on her daughter.

> An emotional cannibal is someone who thinks the only way she can lift herself up is by tearing someone else down.

Madeline has a couple options here. Option #1: Let it go. She can say to herself, "Well, that's just Teresa. I know she has overcome some tough obstacles in her life. She doesn't mean to hurt people when she says stuff like that. She's just desperate to be the center of attention all the time. It's really a shame, because I know she loves God and wants to make a difference. I need to pray for her. Maybe God can use me to bring about some healing in her life. Maybe working on this retreat together will be just the thing she needs to begin viewing herself as a vessel God can use."

Unfortunately, Madeline may go with Option #2. That is, she'll be furious with Teresa. She'll run home, pick up the phone, and call Wendy: "You're not going to believe what Teresa just said to me. When I hang up, I'm calling the pastor and telling him to forget about it. I'm resigning from the retreat committee. If that's the way people at this church want to be, then I'll just go somewhere else!"

Let me change the scenario just slightly, and the real issue will become obvious to you. Let's imagine these two women back at the restaurant. Teresa turns to Madeline and shouts, "Oh, no! You have a purple giraffe growing out of your ear!" Is this going to throw Madeline for an emotional loop? Is she going to run home in an angry snit and start dialing for dollars? Is she going to storm the pastor's office and quit the church? No. She's going to recognize that this is not about her. It's about Teresa. Teresa has serious problems and needs serious prayer. The only reason Madeline flips out is because of her *own* insecurity. If she is confident about who she is, whose she is, and what he has called her to do, then a small thing like an insult won't be enough to send her packing.

The Bible warns us against cannibalistic kinds of behavior: "If you keep on biting and devouring each other, watch out or you will be destroyed by each other" (Gal. 5:14–15).

Hmmmm. Devour? That word sounds familiar. Where have we heard it before? Oh, yeah, now I remember: "Satan prowls around like a roaring lion looking for someone he can devour." Striving for approval (which is a polite way to describe the

> When you are not secure in God's love for you, everything gets blown out of proportion.

193

sin of pride, by the way) and devouring those who prevent you from getting it are sins, fashioned in the pit of hell by the enemy of your soul. He has one mission and one mission only: to render you "ineffective and unproductive in your knowledge of our Lord Jesus Christ" (2 Peter 1:8). Every day that you sit in a pew nursing a grudge, or worse, sit at home licking your wounds, you are giving the enemy the victory. Don't do it.

The solution, in addition to living your life before an audience of one, is developing an unshakable sense of God's love for you. Knowing you are valuable because you *belong* to him, not because you *perform* for him. When you rest securely in his love, it doesn't matter whether or not you bombed that solo. God still loves you.

"So then, just as you received Christ Jesus as Lord, continue to live in him, rooted and built up in him, strengthened in the faith as you were taught, and overflowing with thankfulness" (Col. 2:6–7).

When you are not secure in God's love for you, everything gets blown out of proportion. The vast majority of "Guess What My Church Did to Me" script proposals I've heard are nowhere near Major Motion Picture caliber, although you would never guess it by the way the women involved recount their stories. Because I've been talking about this topic for several months in my speaking ministry, women will actually come up to me and say, "You won't believe this one!" I'm waiting to hear how her church turned out to be a Satanic cult that kidnapped her children and sacrificed them to Lucifer on Halloween. More often than not, it turns out that her church didn't give her the position she wanted, the approval she craved, or the credit she deserved. *Who cares?!?* Does it matter who gets the applause, the thank-you note, and the wing in the church named after them? Isn't this about *Jesus* and *his* kingdom?

No church is perfect. Even the early church, which started so idyllically, was soon embroiled in conflict. In the second chapter of Acts, we find:

> They devoted themselves to the apostles' teaching and to the fellowship, to the breaking of bread and to prayer. Everyone was filled with awe, and many wonders and miraculous signs were done by the apostles. All the believers were together and had everything in common. Selling their possessions and goods, they gave to anyone as he had need. Every day they continued to meet together in the temple courts. They broke bread in their homes and ate together with glad and sincere hearts, praising God and enjoying the favor of all the people. And the Lord added to their number daily those who were being saved.
>
> Acts 2:42–47

Hey, did I just catch you humming "Kumbaya"?

Alas, within a few short years, James was addressing "fights and quarrels," and Paul was writing:

> I plead with Euodia and I plead with Syntyche to agree with each other in the Lord. Yes, and I ask you, loyal yokefellow, help these women who have contended at my side in the cause of the gospel.
>
> Philippians 4:2–3

God is pleading with all of us to get on with the business at hand: the cause of the gospel. I want to return to this topic in the final chapter, but let me give you some food for thought right now. I firmly believe that the broader your perspective on the church as a whole— around the world and throughout history—the better you will feel about your brothers and sisters in Christ. It's only when we focus on the complacent women in our Sunday school class or the troublemakers in every congregation that we become discouraged and want to drop out. No matter how disillusioned you may feel, please remain open to the possibility that other people are just as sincere and well-meaning as you know you are. Here's how Amy Ridgeway, a member of one of my Internet groups, put it:

> I know that there is conflict in all churches, and have experienced it firsthand in painful ways. But after prayer, reflection, time, and patience, I think that God's work will be accomplished through his church, which will never be filled with perfect souls this side of heaven. Still, time after time, regardless of my own emotions, on Sunday morning, I'm there in church, with a whole bunch of other church ladies and church men, each of us in some way not quite up to snuff, but by the time we sing the Doxology and the pastor closes with the benediction, there is still no place I'd rather be, and faults, foibles, hurt feelings, and all the confessed and unconfessed sins of all our hearts—a whole bunch of us unworthy souls somehow find God together.

Having pointed out what's wrong with the church, I want to shift gears and talk about what the church has done *right*. While it is only too true that some real jerks are sitting in church pews, some of the greatest people in the history of the planet were Christians who got up out of those church pews, went forth, and changed the world. In his book *What's So Amazing about Grace?* Philip Yancey paints a panoramic view of the church's accomplishments. With his permission, I've recaptured some of the highlights and thrown in a few extra for good measure. The church needs a few more:

- St. Patrick and his spiritual descendants played a pivotal role in Western history during the period after Rome fell to the barbarians. Thomas Cahill in his book *How the Irish Saved Civilization* details their contribution in copying Scripture and other great works of literature.

- In nineteenth-century England, at least three-quarters of the five hundred new charities formed were organized by Christians, who fought against slavery, debtors' prisons, and child labor, while providing housing, education, and other practical help to the poor.[1]

- The organization founded by William Booth in 1865, the Salvation Army, continues to be one of the most effective churches/charities in the world. It has an annual budget in excess of $1 billion, which is used to "feed the hungry, shelter the homeless, treat addicts and alcoholics and show up first at disaster scenes." The Salvation Army has 1 million people serving in a hundred countries worldwide.[2]

According to Dr. Jerry "Chip" MacGregor, author of *1001 Surprising Things You Should Know about Christianity*, Christians have profoundly impacted the development of Western culture, with a redemptive influence on music (Bach, Handel), classic works of art (Michelangelo, Raphael, Rembrandt), literature (Dostoyevsky, Tolstoy), architecture (think of the great cathedrals), mathematics (Pascal), astronomy (Copernicus, Galileo, Kepler), and science and medicine (John Ray, father of natural history; Gregor Mendel, father of modern genetics).

Lest you are sitting there thinking, *Yeah, that was the good old days*, think again:

- More Christians were martyred for the cause of Christ in the twentieth century than all previous centuries combined (*Voice of the Martyrs* newsletter).
- The current revival in China represents the greatest numerical revival in the history of the church.[3]
- Eastern Europe was set free from the tyranny of communism largely by the courage of Christians such as Polish Catholics who marched in the streets shouting, "We forgive you!" to the government officials who had oppressed them for decades. Meanwhile, East German Christians "lit candles, prayed, and marched in the streets until one night the Berlin Wall collapsed like a rotten dam."[4]
- The hospice movement was founded by a Christian nurse, Dame Cicely Saunders. There are currently two thousand hospices in the United States, and half are overtly run by Christians; many more are staffed by devoted believers.[5]
- Habitat for Humanity was founded by a Christian, Millard Fuller, who invested his personal fortune to launch the organization. It is largely supported by Christians, including former President Jimmy Carter, a devout man who has devoted his retirement years to public service.[6]
- In 2003 alone, Franklin Graham took 5 million shoeboxes, filled with gifts donated by Christians, to disadvantaged children around the world.
- The work of Mother Teresa speaks for itself.

I could go on and on, but I think you get the idea. There are plenty of wonderful Christians doing wonderful work in the world today, even if no one is making Major Motion Pictures about their contributions. Since this is the chapter on church, I've decided to let a few more church ladies have their say. This is from Judy

Lovitt, one of the women who provided input as I wrote this book live online:

> It's usually church people who man the soup kitchens in the ghettos of big cities. It's church youth who go on mission trips to help build, teach, and fellowship with people in third-world countries. Our church has a prison ministry and each week there are new souls brought into the kingdom. Societies don't change from the top down, from government, or from the passing of laws. Societies change from the bottom up, by grass roots movements, by church people who are salt and light in their communities. We *can* bring revival to this nation if we each start with our own hearts.

On the topic of revival in the church, another woman from the online group, Virginia Garrett, added:

> I am saying we need to look around and see what needs to be changed and improved and stick around to change and improve it. If it has to start with the face in the mirror, so be it. I can't pray, "Lord, send a revival to this country. Send a revival to the church" if I'm not willing to pray, "Lord send a revival to this heart of mine" because that is where the real changes and revivals occur.

And I say, Amen, sisters. And to you, my dear reader, I say, "See, I told you there were still some great church people out there. Why don't you go look for a few next Sunday?" Remember:

Ask not what the church can do for you,
Ask what you can do for the church.

199

I'm Flat Broke

He felt terrible for us. He really did. I could see it in his eyes. A leader from our church had telephoned to request a home visit. You have no idea how rare a thing visitors were back then! We were living in West Phila-delphia during the dead of winter, but we didn't have heat in our small apartment. We warned him that we didn't exactly have a cozy place, but he was determined to come anyway.

. When he walked in, I suspect the first thing he no-ticed was that it wasn't a whole lot warmer inside than outside; he opted to keep his coat on (not that he had much of a choice). As he spoke with us, no doubt he could see his breath in the air. He could certainly see ours as we answered his thoughtful questions like, "How do you manage?" So we explained: "Well, obviously we keep our coats on. And we bought a small electric space heater, so we can take turns holding it next to the bathroom sink while we wash our faces and underarms. We wouldn't dream of getting our whole bodies wet. We bought that instant spray shampoo, so we only wash our hair a couple times a week."

Here our visitor took a moment to note down for the prayer team: "Partows—electrocution danger."

"We obviously don't have a car, but the bus route is nearby and we only have to take two buses each way to get to work. What a relief! Before we found jobs downtown, we had to take three buses each way, and *that* was the pits! Unfortunately, we don't get to church that often because that's a bus, a train, and another bus, then we have to walk a mile. Carrying groceries used to be a pain, but we've invested in a wheeled cart to drag home our $25 worth of food each week. If there's not a lot of snow, it works well. Then we can unload, fill it with laundry, and walk to the Laundromat. If we don't finish before dark, walking home is kinda scary. Otherwise, we're doing okay."

He nodded his head and seemed impressed that we were coping so well. If this were the chapter on church, I would mention that we never heard from him again. But this chapter is called "I'm Flat Broke," and I just wanted to let you know that, by American standards, I definitely know what it is to be flat broke. I feel myself slipping into Major Motion Picture mode (which I now realize is always a clear and present danger for me), so I want to move on quickly. But I can't resist just a couple quick anecdotes. For the first few years of her life, my daughter Leah thought *everyone* had to pray their car would start every time they got in it. I remember triumphantly pulling into a gas station with her one day. I say triumphant because we had accomplished our mission for the morning: finding enough money to put gas in the car. (Hey, at least we had a car and not a wheeled cart!) We had searched the entire house: every drawer, every closet, every seat cushion—and came up with 92 cents. It was all the money we had.

I can remember praying for food and being grateful when a neighbor brought over some tomatoes from her garden. I smashed them up, heated them, and put them on top of a 39-cent bag of noodles—and called it an answer to prayer. So I know a little bit about the American version of being down-and-out. But the reality is, even the poorest American knows nothing of famine or the ravages of war. We've never been on the frontline, never witnessed annihilation. We are rich beyond the imaginations of most people who live, or ever have lived, on this planet.

My international travel thus far has been fairly limited, but crossing the border from California into Mexico is something I'll never forget. One minute we were surrounded by the wealth and excess that *is* Southern California: upscale shops, Mercedes Benz, walking Barbie dolls, pampered kids, poodles wearing rhinestones. Then we were transported *someplace else. A whole 'nother world*. Within minutes, I was crying and afraid of the sights, sounds, and smells that overwhelmed my senses. People were rushing up to us, trying to sell things, trying to get a small piece of our wealth. Children stood before me begging, silently pleading. We saw their shacks by the side of the road; saw the cardboard boxes that many called home. Suddenly, I realized how blessed I had always been, even when living in that unheated apartment. At least we *had* real walls, real floors, real *hope*.

Even while I lived in poverty—and yes, I've lived below the American poverty line, which is currently $18,000 per year for a family of four—I always had hope. I could always look around and know, "There's a future in this country *for anyone* with half a brain who's willing to work hard." I knew I had a good mind, the beginnings of a good education, and no fear of hard work. I didn't know how long it would take, but I was convinced that someday, somehow, I could rise above. That's the promise for all of us in twenty-first-century America. It's a promise few have shared.

If you're anything like me, you're still pondering how four people can survive on $4,500 apiece in America today. But the average income in third-world countries is $450 per year. In Haiti, which has the lowest average income, it is $270 per year. Earlier today my eyes happened upon an article entitled "Pay Sent Home Makes Big Difference." Here's an excerpt:

> Salvador Munoz spends long days working in the heat of southern Texas aloe vera fields. Then he works a few odd jobs at night. But the 62-year-old Mexican immigrant doesn't spend much of the roughly $200 he earns each week. Instead, he sleeps at a homeless shelter and gets by on three tacos a day and a visit to the soup kitchen—all so he can send money home for his 13 children.[1]

I just returned from a weekend with the Salvation Army. The next time you are posed with the question "What Would Jesus Do?" and are looking for a short answer, just say, "He'd do what the Salvation Army is doing." And you'd be right. They help alcoholics get sober and drug addicts get clean. They shelter the homeless and protect battered women. They feed the hungry, clothe the naked, heal the sick, and preach the gospel to the lost and hurting. I've worked with many ministries, but few have impressed me more.

Many of the women who attended the Salvation Army weekend event were in the midst of tough circumstances. There was a large group who came from their drug and alcohol treatment programs; others were living in homes for battered women; still others attended Salvation Army programs in rough Washington, D.C., neighborhoods. The

Salvation Army doesn't plant churches next to megamalls in pristine suburban communities—which is not to say we shouldn't be planting churches in such places; obviously, we should. But their heart has always been for "the least of these."

When I spoke, I shared a message of hope with total confidence that God could move these women forward to a better place. Not just "in the sky, by and by," but I'm convinced better opportunities exist right here on earth, at least right here in America right now. At the closing ceremony on Sunday morning, we held hands and cried. I whispered

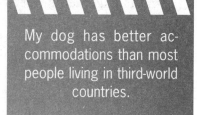

My dog has better accommodations than most people living in third-world countries.

into the ears of more than a few women, "You're gonna make it. I promise. You're gonna make it." They squeezed my hand tighter and cried a little harder. I think some even believed me. With a little job training and a lot of prayer, the promise can come true—because we are Americans and because we are the most blessed nation in the history of civilization.

My dog has better accommodations than most people living in third-world countries. Literally. For a start, she sleeps in the house at night. Not just a mud hut with dirt floors. No, a beautiful, fully furnished house with carpeting. She has her own little bedroom in the form of a large kennel that I've filled with soft blankets. She eats every day without fail and often gets scraps from our table that beggars would kill for. I secretly give her treats. My husband doesn't know that I know this, but he secretly gives her treats, and my kids aren't fooling me, either. It's no wonder the dog is overweight. Just like most Americans.

I've previously written about the time when my well ran dry and we lived for six weeks without running water. In case you're not getting the whole picture, that means our toilets didn't work either. It's one thing to live in a free-and-clear thatched-roof hut without running water; it's another to live in a mortgaged-to-the-hilt-and-you-can-no-longer-afford-it-now-that-you're-a-single-mom house without running water. At least the mud hut residents don't have any pressing book deadlines or speaking engagements but no clean underwear. Talk about Major Motion Picture mode. As I hauled in water from the back of my only friend's husband's pickup truck to force-flush a two-day supply of human waste, I must admit I was ready to turn screenwriter.

But before I sat down to start turning my life story into a based-on-a-true-story movie, I decided to send out an email asking for prayer. I've since learned that this was a mistake. In fact, one woman asked to be removed from my mailing list and specifically mentioned the dry well as the reason. People don't want to know that their favorite author is falling apart at the seams, even when the main reason they like the aforementioned author is because she seems like a regular person. And regular people are regularly falling apart at the seams. But that's another book. This is the one about putting our problems into perspective. Which is what I'm trying to do, if you'll stick with me.

In response to my desperate plea for prayer that God would deliver me from my dire circumstances, I received an email from a reader in Africa who said (I'm paraphrasing), "Earth to Donna. Hello! At least you have access to running water. At least you have the hope that someday it will return. The majority of people in Africa have no such hope. They have to haul water from cholera-infested rivers where hippos go poo."

That certainly put my problems into perspective! Given the choice between my girlfriend's husband's pickup truck in my driveway . . . and a cholera-infested, hippopotamus-inhabited river a three-mile walk down dirt roads, I'll go with the pickup truck any day. Flat broke? Down on my luck? Clearly, I haven't got a clue. Then again flat broke can mean so many different things in America. As my friend Chrissy put it, "Flat broke can mean you're standing on a street corner with a sign, living in a cardboard box with a skinny dog. It could mean you're sleeping on a friend's couch, working three jobs, and living on Top Raman noodles. Or it can mean your husband says you can't go on a cruise again this year. Of course, if my husband ever finds out how much I've *really* charged on all those credit cards, I might end up on that street corner with the skinny dog!"

A turning point in my life occurred when my mom telephoned to let me know my cousin had bumped into the love of my life. Okay, actually, he was just the obsession of my life. But I had spent decades dreaming about this guy, even though I figured he had long since forgotten about me. I figured correctly. He was too busy trying to figure out where his next meal was going to come from. My cousin found him digging through her trash can, homeless, toothless, and, for the real kicker, completely bald. That's down on your luck, American style. But I recently watched a movie, *Romero*, in which an entire village lived *in* an El Salvadoran dump so they could get first pickings from the garbage. That's down on your luck, period.

I've often heard Bible teachers talk about how rich Abraham was. Indeed, the Bible talks about his wealth:

The LORD has blessed my master [Abraham] abundantly, and he has become wealthy. He has given him sheep and

207

cattle, silver and gold, menservants and maidservants, and camels and donkeys.

Genesis 24:35

I'm not entirely sure what I pictured, but I recently watched the TNT Bible Collection version of Abraham's life, and I had an epiphany: rich is one thing; comfortable is another. I don't care how many sheep you have or how many servants you have, when you're living in the Middle Eastern desert, there's not a department store or restaurant in sight. You have to *kill and eat* those adorable little sheep. And that's just for special feasts. Most days, you have bread and water. Maybe some nuts and figs.

I don't think I could live without my shower and bath time. That's about as close to heaven on earth as a body can get. Can you imagine *never* bathing? Can you imagine sharing a tent with a husband who never bathed? Since this is obviously the chapter where the scenario becomes more dire with each sentence, here goes: can you imagine sharing a tent with a husband who never bathes . . . and his three other wives who never bathe? It's getting ugly, isn't it? But are your problems starting to appear a bit more manageable? Good, then I'm earning my keep.

We have no clue what flat broke is all about. Instead, what we are experiencing is that sinking feeling that comes from being in over your head. It's time for the church to get back to basic biblical principles of money management. Oh, what a difference that would make in our lives. First and foremost, Christians need to tithe:

> "Will a man rob God? Yet you rob me.
> "But you ask, 'How do we rob you?'
> "In tithes and offerings. You are under a curse—the whole nation of you—because you are robbing me. Bring

208

the whole tithe into the storehouse, that there may be food in my house. Test me in this," says the LORD Almighty, "and see if I will not throw open the floodgates of heaven and pour out so much blessing that you will not have room enough for it."

Malachi 3:8–10

The simple discipline of living on 10 percent less would do wonders for the average American, not to mention the obvious advantages of putting yourself in a position to be blessed rather than cursed. I recently had a powerful experience in the area of tithing and wrote this letter in response:

May 5, 2004

Dear Gordon,

Thank you for your kind note. It gives me great joy to be a blessing to others, which is why I am writing back to you. As you journey onward in obedience to God's call upon your life, I want you to have just one more reminder of his faithful provision.

Here's "my side of the story." As an author, I only get an official paycheck from my publisher three or four times each year. In between those checks, my income fluctuates quite a bit! On April 26, I gave the tithe from my recent earnings to the Lord. On April 29, Leah brought home your letter. At that moment, I had no income to tithe. Not one penny. My first thought was, *I don't owe God any money!* But then I thought better of it. I told Leah, "I'll just give the whole amount he needs and trust God to provide the income."

That very same day, a television show I had recorded two months earlier was finally broadcast. By the end of the day, I had heard from hundreds of people all over the world who wanted to buy my books or learn more about my ministry. I have done many radio and televi-

209

sion shows, but this was one of the largest responses I have ever received. I sat down today to calculate my earnings since the day I wrote you that check: it was $500 *more* than the income I had offered an "advance tithe" on! Isn't that mind-boggling!?!

Gordon, we can never out-give God. The Bible says the Israelites gave him a tithe of their *FIRSTfruits*. They had no guarantee that the second fruit was coming. Well, let my experience be a witness to you: when we give God our firstfruits, he makes sure we reap a harvest beyond our imagination.

There is no greater joy than living for Jesus!

With love and prayers,

Leah's Mom

When we tithe, we acknowledge that we are serving God rather than money. Jesus said we can't do both:

No servant can serve two masters. Either he will hate the one and love the other, or he will be devoted to the one and despise the other. You cannot serve both God and Money.

Luke 16:13

That last sentence is reiterated again in Matthew 6:24, and it is especially interesting that there it is followed by Jesus's exhortation not to worry:

Do not worry about your life, what you will eat or drink; or about your body, what you will wear. Is not life more important than food, and the body more important than clothes? Look at the birds of the air; they do not sow or reap or store away in barns, and yet your heavenly Father feeds them. Are you not much more valuable

210

than they? Who of you by worrying can add a single hour to his life?

And why do you worry about clothes? See how the lilies of the field grow. They do not labor or spin. Yet I tell you that not even Solomon in all his splendor was dressed like one of these. If that is how God clothes the grass of the field, which is here today and tomorrow is thrown into the fire, will he not much more clothe you, O you of little faith? So do not worry, saying, "What shall we eat?" or "What shall we drink?" or "What shall we wear?" For the pagans run after all these things, and your heavenly Father knows that you need them. But seek first his kingdom and his righteousness, and all these things will be given to you as well.

Matthew 6:25–33

This makes perfect sense, doesn't it? Why don't we tithe? Because we don't truly believe God will take care of us, so we have to worry about ourselves. That's what holds us back from giving more to the kingdom of God, what prevents us from devoting our life to Christian service, and it's what drives us to work longer and longer hours to earn more and more money.

God knows what we are like, and he knows money is a heart-revealing issue. That's why Jesus talked more about money than heaven and hell combined and why there are 125 verses in the Bible addressing our pocketbook. The Bible reminds us, "A man's life does not consist in the abundance of his possessions" (Luke 12:15). Many of Jesus's parables addressed money management, including the parable of the rich fool, which

> Why don't we tithe? Because we don't truly believe God will take care of us, so we have to worry about ourselves.

211

demonstrated the futility of storing up treasures on earth. Instead, Jesus instructed us:

> Do not store up for yourselves treasures on earth, where moth and rust destroy, and where thieves break in and steal. But store up for yourselves treasures in heaven, where moth and rust do not destroy, and where thieves do not break in and steal. For where your treasure is, there your heart will be also.
>
> Matthew 6:19–21

Second, we need to refuse to go into debt. This would have a far-reaching, positive impact on our lifestyles. If you can't buy until you can pay cash, you have to save up. That's what Americans did for centuries. There's a scene in *The Homecoming* that captures convictions that were once almost universal in this country. It's Christmas Eve during the Depression, and the father has not yet returned from his job in a neighboring city. The mother walks into town to buy some sugar, and the shop owner tries to convince her to use store credit to buy a doll for her daughter. She looks at him as if he had just suggested she put rattlesnakes in their Christmas stockings and says solemnly, "This family does not buy on credit."

It's a policy more of us should adopt. As you are saving up to buy a particular item, you have an opportunity to do something most of us have forgotten how to do: think it over. It's the opposite of impulse buying, mindlessly throwing "stuff" into your shopping cart at the mall or on the Internet. If we had to save up and ponder our purchases, we wouldn't have closets filled with clothes we never wear. My uncle lived with my parents until he died in 1973, and if I'm not mistaken, he had exactly five sets of clothing.

Speaking of clothes, your wardrobe is covered under the universal 80/20 rule (also called the Pareto principle).

That is, you probably wear 20 percent of your clothes 80 percent of the time. I know I do. Which begs the question: why did you buy the other 80 percent? Because you could. Well, at least you thought you could, thanks to your handy-dandy credit card. A friend recently quipped that her grandfather, a banker, was on hand for the launch of the charge-a-plate and declared, "It will be the ruination of us all." He was absolutely right.

The average American household has $30,000 in credit card debt. If they only pay the minimum amount each month, they will be paying it off for the next twenty-five years. In the end, they will have paid $500,000 for $30,000 worth of stuff.[2] That's assuming the stuff was worth that much in the first place, which of course it wasn't.

Let me tell you my story, because I think it's indicative of the way many Americans get into trouble. In 1992, my family and I moved to Arizona in search of a fresh start on life. With the proceeds from the sale of our small, three-bedroom trailer in New Jersey, we were able to buy a brand-new home in a brand-new housing development. When we were house hunting back East, the houses in our price range were at least thirty years old and run-down, so when we walked through the model homes in Arizona, we couldn't believe our eyes. We thought we had died and gone to heaven. Then we lived through our first summer in Arizona, and it felt like a different place entirely, but that's off the subject.

The first thing that dawned on us after moving into our 2,500-square-foot home (more than twice the size of our previous house), was that we didn't have nearly enough furniture to fill it. The most embarrassing part was the front room, which was designed with huge, wraparound bay windows so everyone could see into your beautiful dining room. Unfortunately, we didn't have any dining-room furniture; our last house had only a humble kitchen.

213

So the neighbors looked in and saw our empty dining room instead. Adjacent to the dining room was a "formal living room." We didn't have any formal living-room furniture either. When you walk through the model homes, everything is fabulously decorated. Somehow, you never stop to think, *Hey, wait a minute. It's not going to look so great with my old yard sale junk in it!*

Yard sale junk is exactly what we had. Even the treasured knickknacks and "personal touches" I had so proudly displayed in our former home now seemed hickish and out of place. I suddenly felt like a social outcast, especially as all the neighbors busily worked to decorate the interior of their brand-spanking-new houses. Interior decorating is particularly important in Arizona because on the outside, all the houses look alike. In our subdivision, hundreds of houses were built with only three different models to choose from—and they were all painted the exact same color on the outside. Even the yards looked exactly the same, because they were planted and maintained by hardworking Mexican immigrants in return for the $35 per month association fee everyone had to pay. Those poor immigrants were probably paid exactly $35 a month, and you can bet they sent half of it home. I wonder if they considered themselves flat broke?

Anyway, if you were going to make a personal statement to tell the neighbors who you were, you had better do it inside. Within a week of moving in, we were bombarded with flyers from window treatment companies. I honestly had never heard of "window treatments" before I moved to Arizona. But since our new house was filled with giant windows, not one of which had so much as a curtain rod to protect us from baking in the sun, we had no choice but to fork over two months' salary to one of our new neighbors. She had launched her very own window treatment company to capitalize on our mutual predicament. Naturally, we didn't have two months' salary sitting around, but we did have our credit card, and she gladly accepted it.

I think you can guess the rest. We went to a buy-now-pay-later furniture store. Cha-ching. We hired another neighbor, who had started an interior decorating business, to help us spruce up the place. Cha-ching. By then, our house started looking so good that we couldn't help but notice that we had the wrong car. Cha-ching. Our clothes were outdated. Cha-ching. Our daughter needed a life-sized Barbie doll. Cha-ching.

Our neighborhood was filled with women who had "no choice" but to work. Once you are working, you have "no choice" but to buy work clothes. Cha-ching. You need childcare, and your kids need a wardrobe. Cha-ching. When you work hard all day, who has time to cook dinner? Grab something on the way home or take the family out to dinner. Between sitting at a desk all day and eating fast food, you start gaining weight, so you have to join a gym. One look around and you realize you need workout clothes. Thank God for credit cards. Alas, you never actually go to the gym, but you signed a two-year agreement, so they keep charging your credit card, even though your workout wear sits permanently in your new gym bag. Time to try a diet. Off you go to Jenny Craig, just $20 a month plus the cost of food. Once you've lost all that weight, it's time for new clothes and a cruise vacation. You've worked hard and you deserve it!

I would keep saying cha-ching, but I don't want to be redundant. I think you know what I'm driving at here; I think you know because many of you are on the same treadmill. Or at least you know a few people who are, and maybe you can ask them to read this chapter. If they want to buy the whole book, they can send me their credit card number.

I tried to get off the treadmill by moving out of the subdivision and into the mountains. Unfortunately, the simple life is much more complicated and far more expensive than most people imagine. I finally did get completely out of debt last year, and it was a fabulous feeling. Like the weight of the world was lifted off my shoulders. Sadly, being debt free only lasted for three months. Long story. Major Motion Picture–worthy, too, but I'm not going to tell it right now. (There's the cliff-hanger. Be sure to read the next book and find out how Donna Partow got back into debt!)

I can literally feel the burden of debt weighing me down and pulling me deeper into its clutches. It sucks the life out of me. I truly believe it's a snare of the enemy. He wants to keep us on the run so we can never experience God's peace. Remember chapter 4?

You should know by now that I have my share of faults. Lord knows I do. But among the worst is my constant recitation of the phrase "I *have* to work." I say it to my kids all the time. "I *have* to work." Worst of all, I've said it to myself so long that I'm actually starting to believe it, "I *have* to work." Would one of you love me enough to come over here and smack me! The only reason I have to work so hard is because I am in debt. In truth, I am enslaved to the mountain of stuff I have accumulated. Now I have to pay for it and take care of it. It's astonishing how quickly I got back into this mess even after vowing never to go into debt again.

I'm not alone. According to the American Bankruptcy Institute, "Each year since 1996, more than a million Americans have filed for personal bankruptcy." In 2003, one out of every seventy-three American households declared bankruptcy, involving a total of $7.9 trillion in assets. In Utah, it was even higher: nearly half of all households declared bankruptcy.[3] Tell me if this thought has ever crossed your mind: *I'll buy a new wardrobe, take a vacation, max out all my credit cards, and buy two new cars. Then I'll declare bankruptcy and never pay for any of it!* How cool would that be? That's "getting away with something" big-time. I just love feeling like I'm getting away with something, don't you? What, you never thought that? Does anyone? Do people honestly sit down and plan, in advance, to file for bankruptcy? Maybe some do, I honestly don't know. I think most people just get in over their heads and see no other way to escape. They experience a sudden catastrophic illness or lose their jobs. Next thing you know, they are careening toward financial disaster.

Financial stress is considered the #1 factor contributing to divorce in America today. Fifty-seven percent of divorced couples in the United States cited financial problems as the primary reason for the demise of their marriage, according to a survey conducted by Citibank.[4] Financial stress is also a major cause of marital disharmony, even above sex and the kids.

I recently got a small taste of what people go through before they hire that bankruptcy attorney and "take the easy way out" of their miry pit. We purchased a pickup truck last year because we were certain my teenager was on the way to the Olympics, so we needed a truck and horse trailer immediately. I don't think she's even looked at that horse since the day we bought the truck. Now this is the embarrassing part. We didn't have enough money in our checkbook when the first two payments came due. However, my home equity line of credit has a checkbook. So I started paying my bills using my line-of-credit checks. Friends, this is *not* the recommended course of action.

Anyway, one day I got a call from a bill collector who said I had yet to make a single payment on the pickup truck, and if I didn't pay right then, they were coming to take it away. He said he could take my check number and bank-routing number right over the phone. For my convenience, of course. I agreed. Two days later, the phone began ringing off the hook. They had both my home and cell phone numbers. Sometimes both were ringing at once. The minute I would hang up, they would call again. Every time, it was a different person demanding the entire story all over again. Whenever I tried to end the phone conversation, they would say, "Fine, we're on our way to repossess that truck." I kept trying to explain that I had made the payments. They wouldn't listen. They called day and night, even on weekends. I thought I was going insane.

I finally figured out the mix-up. They didn't accept line-of-credit checks, but rather than telling me that, they just said they never received any payments. Around this time, I finally received a royalty check and was able to pay a nice chunk against the truck. I tried to imagine what it would feel like to have dozens of bill collectors calling me all day long. Tried to imagine if I was truly in over my head and literally couldn't pay. Tried to imagine if my husband had lost his job and I couldn't find work, and we were slipping deeper and deeper, with a mountain of debt on top of us and no cash reserves under us. That's the reality for countless Americans.

Which brings us to the third thing we must do to overcome the ridiculous notion that we are "flat broke." We need to set aside some money for a rainy day. Because even though you may not be flat broke—not yet—the mental weight of knowing *how quickly* you *could be* flat broke is a very real problem. According to research provided by Steve Moore, Vice President of Broadcasting for Crown Financial Ministries, only one in five workers has enough savings set aside to last two months without a regular income. In December 2004, there were more than eight million people out of work in America and the average person will remain unemployed for nearly twenty weeks.[5] You do the math. In fact, you might want to do the math for your own family before you start accumulating that mountain of debt. That should be incentive enough to pay cash.

And while you are saving up to buy things, you may just realize you don't want them that badly after all. So you'll buy less stuff. Better quality, but less of it. As a result, you might just be able to afford staying home with your children, if that's what you want to do. Since you are home, you'll be able to cook nutritious meals rather than the fat-salt-and-chemical-laden garbage most Americans live on. You won't gain weight, so you won't suffer from the countless degenerative diseases created (or at least aggravated by) excess weight. You'll have more time to take good care of your body. Your whole lifestyle will be impacted in a positive way. You might even rediscover free family entertainment like old-fashioned board games or reading aloud together. These things don't cost a penny. No charge card needed. These are simple pleasures, and as a result, your life will be more pleasurable. Since you'll already be happy, you won't have to spend money just to feel happy.

The reality is, no matter how much money you make, you'll always need "a little bit more" to live on. I used to live on $100 a week; now I'm "flat broke" earning many times that amount. Whatever you make, that's what it takes to make you *almost* happy. I knew a couple living in a $2 million home, and they constantly argued over family finances. It's not a money issue; it's a heart issue, which is why the tenth commandment says, "Do not covet."

Don't want what other people have; be thankful for what you have. Unfortunately, the entire American economic system depends on covetousness—convincing us that we need ER. Not the TV show. Not even a visit to the local hospital. No, I mean the suffix "er." Whiter teeth, fresher breath, faster cars, smarter kids, a higher position within the company, and America's favorite:

bigger! Bigger hamburgers, bigger houses, bigger cars, bigger boobs. Personally, all I want is smaller thighs. Just moments ago, I was getting dressed and thinking, once again, about how much I hate my thighs. I am truly obsessed. Yes indeed, if only I had thinner thighs, then I could be happy. But as long as I'm dragging these masses of flesh around, how can I possibly experience the joy of the Lord? I hate to admit this, but not a day goes by that I don't look at other women's thighs in search of

> The entire American economic system depends on covetousness—convincing us that we need ER—faster, higher, bigger.

just *one woman* whose thighs are disproportionater than mine. Okay, my dictionary says that's not a real word. But let me tell you, I know I could find contentment if I knew there was someone, anyone, with more disproportionate thighs than me! Happy now? Me neither.

It's deception, friends. Deception. Do you know who the deceiver is? That's why the Bible says,

> But godliness with contentment is great gain. For we brought nothing into the world, and we can take nothing out of it. But if we have food and clothing, we will be content with that. People who want to get rich fall into temptation and a trap and into many foolish and harmful desires that plunge men into ruin and destruction. For the love of money is the root of all kinds of evil. Some people, eager for money, have wandered from the faith and pierced themselves with many griefs.
>
> 1 Timothy 6:6–10

You are not flat broke. If you were truly flat broke, you wouldn't be reading this book right now. You'd be living in a cardboard box, wondering where your next meal was coming from. But you may be at the end of your rope, and as they say, that's a great place to find God. Get out of debt and stay out. Stop buying stuff you don't need. Slow down and enjoy the simple things. Be thankful for what you do have, rather than obsessing constantly about what you don't have. One thing you might do is read books and watch movies set in simpler times. Even an old episode of *Little House on the Prairie* will do.

Even though my publisher for this book is sure to pitch a fit when they find out this next excerpt came to me over the Internet, it's so good they'll just have to get over it:

One day a father of a very wealthy family took his son on a trip to the country with the firm purpose of showing his son how poor people live. They spent a couple of days and nights on the farm of what would be considered a very poor family.

On their return from their trip, the father asked his son, "How was the trip?"

"It was great, Dad."

"Did you see how poor people live?" the father asked.

"Oh yeah," said the son.

"So, tell me, what did you learn from the trip?" asked the father.

The son answered: "I saw that we have one dog and they had four. We have a pool that reaches to the middle of our garden and they have a creek that has no end. We have imported lanterns in our garden and they have the stars at night. Our patio reaches to the front yard and they have the whole horizon. We have a small piece of land to live on and they have fields that go beyond our sight. We buy our food, but they grow theirs. We have walls around our property to protect us, they have friends

221

to protect them." The boy's father was speechless. Then his son added, "Thanks, Dad, for showing me how poor we are."

Isn't perspective a wonderful thing? We are *all* richly blessed.

12

The *Real* Major Motion Picture

Throughout the pages of this book, we've discovered that many of us create our own problems—or at least exacerbate them—by acting as if we were starring in a Major Motion Picture. We mistakenly turn our mellow dramas into melodramas and make life harder than it has to be. In this final chapter, I want us to look at our lives from a completely different perspective: God's. There actually is a Major Motion Picture, a Grand Melodrama, being played out upon the earth. There truly is a completely villainous villain named Satan, and a perfectly good Hero with plans to come to our rescue. God is working out his plan of redemption for all mankind, and he has handpicked you to be part of it. The importance of the Grand Drama can never be exaggerated. It can't be blown out of proportion. In fact, the more focused you are on the real Drama, the easier it is to keep your melodramas mellow dramas.

I often challenge my audiences with this question: Is there something God has called you to do, but since he hasn't given you all the answers up front, you refuse to take a step of faith?

Let me give you an example of what I mean. Several years ago, I had a foster child who wanted to go on a mission trip to Africa. The mission agency instructed her that the first thing she needed to do was send away for a pair of construction boots, put them on immediately, and wear them every day to break them in. So she sent away for the boots. Then she sent out her prayer letter to raise the $5,000 it was going to cost to get her there. And guess what? Not much happened! So when the boots finally arrived, she put them in the back of her closet with the tags still on them. Since God didn't give her all the answers up front, she refused to put on those boots. They literally sat in the back of her closet for three solid months with the tags still on them.

We'll get back to her boots later, but for now here's the question for you: Have you put on your boots yet? Or are they in the back of the closet with the tags still on them? Is there something God has called you to do, but since he hasn't given you all the answers up front, you refuse to take a step of faith? Some of you are thinking, *Actually, no. I don't think there is anything I've been called to do. I'm just here taking up pew space.* Or maybe you think, *I'm here because my parents were Christians. If they were Buddhists, I'd probably be a Buddhist. But we've always been Baptist, so I'm Baptist.*

However, I don't think you've accidentally shown up on the set of this Major Motion Picture. I think you've been handpicked by God to join the cast. It's a little scary though. Do you ever look around your church and think: *If these are the ones God picked, I'd hate to be trapped in a room filled with the ones who didn't make the casting cut . . . ?*[1]

Nevertheless, Jesus said: "You did not choose me, but I chose you" (John 15:16). You may not have a starring role in God's Grand Design for Mankind, but you certainly have a vital part to play. No one else can read from the script you've been given; no one else can portray you. Kate Winslet no doubt thought she was lucky to land the lead in *Titanic*, but the person playing the smallest role in God's epic adventure will receive far greater rewards and accolades that last throughout eternity.

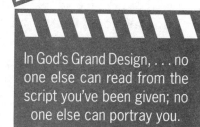

In God's Grand Design, . . . no one else can read from the script you've been given; no one else can portray you.

I don't know about you, but I rejoice in the thought that the Ultimate Casting Director handpicked me for the only Major Motion Picture that truly matters. That's because I've always felt like the last person in the world anyone would ever pick. Do you remember dreading PE class with that whole "dividing into teams" drill? I was almost always one of the last kids picked. It went something like this:

"We're not gonna take Donna—you take Donna."

"No, we're not gonna take her."

"Tell you what. We'll give you Donna and a 10-point lead."

"Forget it."

"We'll give you Donna, a 10-point lead, and the new aluminum bat."

"Well, okay. I guess we can just put her out in left field."

Of course, many people would say I've been out in left field ever since! I know what it feels like to be the "un-picked one." Maybe you do, too. So I was thrilled beyond belief to know that the God of the Universe

225

had picked me. Not only do I believe that all of us are handpicked by God, I believe:

God has a specific part for you to play in his Major Motion Picture!

Let me give you some biblical examples of what I'm talking about here. Samuel was handpicked by God and given a specific part to play:

> Then the LORD called Samuel.
> Samuel answered, "Here I am." And he ran to Eli and said, "Here I am; you called me."
> But Eli said, "I did not call; go back and lie down." So he went and lay down.
> Again the LORD called, "Samuel!" And Samuel got up and went to Eli and said, "Here I am; you called me."
> "My son," Eli said, "I did not call; go back and lie down."
> Now Samuel did not yet know the LORD: The word of the LORD had not yet been revealed to him.
> The LORD called Samuel a third time, and Samuel got up and went to Eli and said, "Here I am; you called me."
> Then Eli realized that the LORD was calling the boy. So Eli told Samuel, "Go and lie down, and if he calls you, say, 'Speak, LORD, for your servant is listening.'" So Samuel went and lay down in his place.
> The LORD came and stood there, calling as at the other times, "Samuel! Samuel!"
> Then Samuel said, "Speak, for your servant is listening."
>
> 1 Samuel 3:4–10

Throughout Samuel's lifetime, he served as a prophet of God, speaking forth the words God gave him.

Jeremiah was handpicked by God and given a specific part to play:

The word of the LORD came to me, saying,

"Before I formed you in the womb I knew you,
before you were born I set you apart;
I appointed you as a prophet to the nations."

Jeremiah 1:4–5

Isaiah was handpicked by God and given a specific part to play:

Before I was born the LORD called me. . . .
And now the LORD says . . .
"It is too small a thing for you to be my servant
to restore the tribes of Jacob
and bring back those of Israel I have kept.
I will also make you a light for the Gentiles,
that you may bring my salvation to the ends of the
earth."

Isaiah 49:1, 5–6

Okay, that's all Old Testament. How about the New Testament? Funny you should ask, because I was just getting there:

As Jesus was walking beside the Sea of Galilee, he saw two brothers, Simon called Peter and his brother Andrew. They were casting a net into the lake, for they were fishermen. "Come, follow me," Jesus said, "and I will make you fishers of men."

Matthew 4:18–19

Simon Peter and Andrew were handpicked by God and given specific parts to play. But they weren't alone!

227

How about the apostle Paul? Jesus hunted him down on the Damascus Road and told him:

> Now get up and go into the city, and you will be told what you must do.
>
> Acts 9:6

Sounds like the man is going to be given a pretty specific part to play, does it not? Here's how Paul later described it:

> God, who set me apart from birth and called me by his grace, was pleased to reveal his Son in me so that I might preach him among the Gentiles.
>
> Galatians 1:15–16

Set apart from birth? Sounds like he was handpicked. Why? So that he might preach the gospel to the Gentiles. That's certainly a specific part to play.

If you are a follower of Jesus Christ, I'm absolutely convinced it is because God handpicked you. Now don't get paranoid on me and start thinking, *What if he didn't pick me?* If you're reading this book, you're in the script. But maybe you think you're nothing more than an extra in this Major Motion Picture. Your only role is to fill in some vacancies in the pews. Did God cast your role just because he thought you might look good sitting in church? Many people act as if they believe John 15:16 says, "You did not choose me, but I chose you to sit . . . to sit and make notes concerning what's wrong with everyone else." But that's not what it says. It says, "You did not choose me, but I chose you and appointed you to go . . ."

The script calls for each and every one of us to *GO*, never to sit. God handpicked you because he has a very

228

specific part for you to play. No one else can do it quite like you can.

This Major Motion Picture is an epic battle, pitting the forces of God against the forces of Satan. The battlefield is earth. But this isn't Star Wars; it's the real thing. There's a spiritual battle being waged on this planet. For reasons we may never understand, there are rules of engagement that God has apparently chosen to honor. Of course, God versus Satan is really not a fair fight. Satan is not the equal of God; if anything he is on par with Michael and Gabriel, the archangels. Who knows? Maybe God just wanted to level the playing field, so he said, "Okay, Satan, you want to have it out with me over planet Earth? Let's get to it. Not only am I going to beat you, I'm going to beat you with one hand tied behind my back. You know those creatures you despise more than anything else I have created? Those human beings? I'm going to beat you doing only what I can accomplish through them." And when God pulls it off—and we know he will in the end—it will be the ultimate humiliation for Satan.

We know that no one and nothing can limit God. Make no mistake about that. God is the sovereign creator and sustainer of all things. But consider this passage from Ezekiel 22:30–31:

> I looked for a man among them who would build up the wall and stand before me in the gap on behalf of the land so I would not have to destroy it, but I found none. So I will pour out my wrath on them and consume them with my fiery anger, bringing down on their own heads all they have done, declares the Sovereign LORD.

Isn't it somewhat astonishing that God would describe himself as Sovereign Lord just one sentence after using the words "have to"? Doesn't that seem like a contradic-

229

tion? If God is sovereign, how can he "have to" do or not do anything? Because of our indifference. Because we refuse to play the part God planned for us. Standing in the gap has long been considered a metaphor for prayer. In this passage, God clearly states that he needs someone to play the role of pray-er. According to E. M. Bounds, noted nineteenth-century authority on the subject of prayer:

> God has chosen to limit His actions on this earth to those things done in direct response to believing prayer.[2]

Doesn't it follow, then, that most of our lines in this script should be uttered in the form of a prayer? Have you ever had the experience of feeling prompted—or even burdened—to pray for someone? I once read of a woman who woke up in the middle of the night, impressed with the need to pray urgently for her daughter's safety. As it turns out, at that very hour her daughter, a missionary in Africa, was in a stalled vehicle with her children—directly in the path of a stampeding herd of elephants. Why did God wake up this woman in the middle of the night *to pray*? Why not let her enjoy a good night's sleep and simply redirect the charging elephants *without* her prayer? Because "God has chosen to limit His actions on this earth to those things done in direct response to believing prayer." We have a part to play in God's Major Motion Picture. Our prayers truly make a difference.

Here's the way I believe prayer works. God is always watching over every corner of the earth. He sees a situation that is out of line with his will and decides to intervene. But wait! He had chosen to limit his actions on the earth to those things he can accomplish through his people. So "the eyes of the LORD range throughout the earth to strengthen those whose hearts are fully committed to him" (2 Chron. 16:9). He looks around and sees a believer on her knees. Someone who has set aside her prayer list (see chapter 6) and is sitting quietly, listening intently for God's voice.

Let's imagine the obedient woman is *you*. Into the silence God speaks, sharing his very heart with you. As you begin to pray, you literally *release* God into the situation. I love the word picture Frank Peretti used in his book *This Present Darkness* where he portrayed prayer as fuel for angels' wings. What a powerful image. God is ready and eager to bring about his kingdom upon this earth; but he has instructed *us* to *pray* that his kingdom will come and his will be done, on earth as it is in heaven. Was God serious when he gave us the assignment to pray? I believe he was. God will prompt us to pray; he will guide our prayer; but he won't do the praying for us.

Most of our lines in this script should be uttered in the form of a prayer.

Something else happens, too. As God begins to share his heart with you, a theological marvel unfolds. It's called snookering. In the original Greek, it means "You are getting up out of this pew." Yes, indeed, when you listen in prayer, God will snooker you. Sometimes I think we read the Bible in a more serious tone of voice than God intends. Let me explain what I mean. Whenever people quote "WHOM SHALL I SEND?" they always sound like James Earl Jones. And Isaiah is portrayed as *volunteering* to go. I don't think that was it at all. I think God was snookering him.

I want you to imagine you're standing in the kitchen with your five-year-old, who has made a huge mess.

You aren't angry with him, but there is work to be done and he is the one who needs to do it, so you say, "Oh my, look at this mess, Jeremy. Don't you think someone should clean it up?"

"Yes, Mommy."

"Well, whom do you think we could get to clean it up? Can you think of someone?"

If Jeremy is the only one sitting there, no doubt he'll take the hint and say, "I don't know, Mommy . . . maybe . . . me?"

"Exactly! Okay, Jeremy, get to work!"

God had every intention of sending Isaiah; Isaiah just didn't know it yet. I find it absolutely astonishing that the passage we read from Isaiah, where it says God chose him for this assignment long before he was born, doesn't come until Isaiah chapter 49! It was only later (in the closing scene, if you will) that Isaiah was able to look back on his life and realize: Aha! So *that's* what God was up to! At this point in the Major Motion Picture, God is simply asking Isaiah a rhetorical question:

> Then I heard the voice of the Lord saying, "Whom shall I send? And who will go for us?"
> And I said, "Here am I. Send me!"
>
> Isaiah 6:8

God has a specific part for you to play, as well. You may not know what it is at this very moment. But some day, when you come to the end of your life, I hope you will be able to look back and say, "Yes, now I see. This is what God had in mind all along." As you listen in prayer, God will invite you to step into that place of ministry that he prepared for you before the foundation of the world.

232

For it is by grace you have been saved, through faith—and this not from yourselves, it is the gift of God—not by works, so that no one can boast. For we are God's workmanship, created in Christ Jesus to do good works, which God prepared in advance for us to do.

Ephesians 2:8–10

God not only wants you to pray, he wants you to become part of the answer. God looks down upon this earth and sees:

- A marriage falling apart at your church
- A latchkey child in your neighborhood surfing the Internet, in grave danger
- A teenager in your daughter's class starving herself to be beautiful
- A message to be proclaimed
- A song to be sung
- An unsent missionary
- A persecuted church
- An unreached people

God asks, "Who will go?" Well, it will probably be somebody who gets snookered into praying "Your kingdom come, your will be done on earth as it is in heaven." When God was ready to bring me into the kingdom, he didn't pick up the phone. He laid it on someone's heart to call me. Nor did God take human form so he could pick me up and drive me to that retreat center. Although I guess he could have sent an angel, he chose a young man. That young man picked up the phone, then picked me up in his parents' station wagon.

Whom is God laying on your heart? Whom do you need to pick up and take to a place where she can encounter God in a life-changing way? I'm so thankful

233

my friend was praying and got snookered into reaching out to me.

If we really believe that we have been chosen by God to play a part in this Major Motion Picture, why do we just sit in the pews, refusing to get involved? What holds us back? What is holding *you* back? Why haven't you put on your boots? Why are they sitting in the back of your closet with the tags still on them?

I can't answer that question for all of you. But I'm convinced the #1 reason why people refuse to put on the boots is because we don't feel qualified. You know why? Because we've blown it. We've made foolish choices. And we think those choices mean that we have been disqualified from serving God. That's what happened to me.

I spent so many years of my life feeling like I had completely blown it. I thought, *Yes, God had a part for me to play. But I made foolish choices and ruined everything. Now there's no possible way I could ever be of any use in the kingdom of God.* But eventually, God was able to deliver me out of the mess I had made of my life. There's no denying that I have made some very foolish choices, but . . .

Your foolish choices do NOT negate the call of God upon your life.

Think about Moses for a minute. God literally handpicked him up out of the Nile River. It's interesting to note that he did not reveal the "why" to Moses for forty years. So if you've been sitting in church for forty years and you're not clear what your role is, you're in good company. When God finally let Moses in on his plan to liberate the people of Israel, what is the first thing Moses did? He blew it. He flew off the handle and murdered an Egyptian. That may play well in a Cecil B. DeMille epic, but in real life, it wasn't exactly a smart choice.

234

But let me ask you something. When Moses blew it, did God cast someone else to play his part? No, he gave him a forty-year time-out in the desert to reconsider. When Moses finally appears before Pharaoh, he is eighty years old. Some might think he was carrying a cane so he could turn it into a snake. Wrong! The cane was not a prop. He was carrying a cane because he was an old man. And the reason he was an old man was because he blew it the first time God gave him the assignment.

And I will guarantee you, during most of those years he spent tending sheep out in the desert, he thought God was through with him. Was God through with him? Obviously not. His foolish choices just gave God the opportunity to convince Moses that this assignment had nothing to do with him and the great things he could do for God.

When I first moved to Arizona in 1992, I lived in the Phoenix area (also called the Valley of the Sun). And of course, my favorite place to go was always the Christian bookstore. Then I moved up to the mountains to my little cabin in the woods. Several years after my move, someone gave me a gift certificate to one of the Christian bookstores in the Valley. I hopped in my car and headed down the mountain. I was the happiest woman on the planet, because I was on my way to spend money without actually spending my own money. I'm convinced that must be what is meant by achieving nirvana.

I was driving along in my car, singing praise to the Lord. Life was wonderful. Then I suddenly realized I wasn't so sure I knew where I was going. I started slowing down at every intersection, searching every strip mall for evidence of the Christian bookstore. If you know anything about the Valley of the Sun, you know that when you pull a stunt like that, the people behind you will go nuts. They were beeping their horns and yelling at me, but I didn't care. I was thinking, *I am on a mission for God here. Back off, Buster!*

I must confess the joy of the Lord went right out the window. This scenario—me slowing down at every intersection while my fellow drivers pitched a fit—continued for several more miles. Then finally, in complete exasperation, I made an illegal U-turn. I backtracked for what seemed like an eternity, slowing down at every intersection. People beeping, me panicking. Same routine. At that point, I was close to having a nervous breakdown. I pulled into a little park, and there was a guy putting on rollerblades. I asked him, "Do you know where Hayden intersects with Roosevelt?" Well, he didn't know. But he had a map, and unlike most men, he was willing to use it.

He took out the map, found the street, looked at me, and said, "You're not lost. You're doing fine. Just get right back out on this road, head south another ten minutes, and you'll be all set."

Okay, the joy of the Lord had returned!

I started driving along, and I got right to the intersection where I had made the illegal U-turn. And what to my wondering eyes should appear? The roof of the Christian bookstore! I had been in my car for almost two hours and had stopped two minutes short of my destination. *I had been on the right path all along, but so shaken by doubt that I was no better off than someone who was truly lost.*

I'll say that again. I had been on the right path all along, but so shaken by doubt that I was no better off than someone who was truly lost. If that's not a metaphor for the Christian life as most of us live it, I don't know what is. We're on the right path. We're on the way to heaven. But so shaken by doubt that we're no better off than people who are truly lost. Slowing down when we should be full speed ahead. Making illegal U-turns when the going gets tough.

Let's go back to Moses. We left him an old man in Pharaoh's court. He was finally on course to fulfill the call of God upon his life. The cameras were rolling and the Israelites were marching out to the Promised Land, when suddenly they encountered a seemingly impossible obstacle: the Red Sea. At that moment, with the Egyptian army closing in from behind, the most tempting thing in the world would have been for Moses to make the old "illegal U-turn." To go back, groveling to Pharaoh, "Well, I know I told you I was on assignment from God, but you know, I'm not so sure. I think I may be drinking too much caffeine lately. Sometimes, with too many carbs, I get a little loopy. This couldn't possibly be God's idea, because if it were God's idea I wouldn't encounter any obstacles. Everything would just be smooth sailing."

But Moses resisted the temptation to make that illegal U-turn. And I think I know why. I think he grabbed hold of a truth, standing there that day. A truth some of you may need to grab hold of for yourselves. I think Moses knew that God had not pulled him from the river . . . just to drown him in the sea.

Moses knew God had work for him to do, and he was going to press on in faith until the task was completed. It's obvious that Moses had learned his lesson. This time, he didn't try to take matters into his own hands. He knew, after forty years in the desert, that there was nothing within him that could get the job done for God. Instead, what did he do? He held up his cane.

His cane was the symbol of his disqualifications. He carried a cane because he was an old man. He was an old man because he blew it the first time God handed him this script. So he held up the cane and said, "God, I can't. But you can, and I believe you will."

What is the symbol of your disqualification? I would urge you, right now, to hold it up before God. Hold it up over the obstacles in your life and declare, "God, this is why the world says I can't serve you. I can't. But you can, and I believe you will."

I'm absolutely convinced that the only reason God chose to place me in such a prominent ministry position is to say to all the holier-than-thou Christians who pride themselves on keeping the rules: "I will use whomever I choose as my vessel, and there's not a *thing* you can do about it!"

Moses had made an incredibly foolish choice. He chose to commit murder. That's pretty intense. We would surely pull his books off the shelves of the Christian bookstores for that one! But, was God through with Moses? Was Moses disqualified from ever being used by God? Then what makes you think God is through with you?

God does not call the qualified. He qualifies the called.

The only qualification any of us ever have is the finished work of Christ on the cross. It is on that basis alone that we have been declared competent as ministers of a new covenant. I'll tell you what, the minute you think you're qualified, you are on your way to the desert to tend some sheep for a while. And God will keep you out in that wilderness until you can get your head on straight and figure out who the real star of this Major Motion Picture really is. It's not about us; it's about him.

God did not call you because you were qualified. He called you because he has a specific part for you to play in this Grand Drama. No one else on the planet can do it quite like you.

Let's go back to the boots. God had given my foster daughter a specific assignment, to go to Africa and serve him there. But she needed to raise $5,000, and that just seemed so overwhelming. So big! So impossible! Then one day it occurred to me that there was another young person in the Bible whom God called for a specific assignment. His name was Gideon:

> The angel of the LORD came and sat down under the oak in Ophrah that belonged to Joash the Abiezrite, where his son Gideon was threshing wheat in a winepress to keep it from the Midianites. When the angel of the LORD appeared to Gideon, he said, "The LORD is with you, mighty warrior."
>
> "But sir," Gideon replied, "if the LORD is with us, why has all this happened to us? Where are all his wonders that our fathers told us about when they said, 'Did not the LORD bring us up out of Egypt?' But now the LORD has abandoned us and put us into the hand of Midian."
>
> The LORD turned to him and said, "Go in the strength you have and save Israel out of Midian's hand. Am I not sending you?"
>
> "But Lord," Gideon asked, "how can I save Israel? My clan is the weakest in Manasseh, and I am the least in my family."
>
> The LORD answered, "I will be with you."
>
> Judges 6:11–16

I noticed that God doesn't argue with Gideon, trying to convince him that he *is* qualified. Instead, he poses a simple question: "Am I not sending you?" That's all we need to know. If God's not sending you, do the world a favor and stay home. Nothing is worse than a Christian running a self-assigned errand for God. But if God is sending you, no one can stop you. Because it's never about the one who's going. It's about the one who's sending.

So let me ask you something:

Who's sending you? Whose Major Motion Picture is this anyway?

It is not about your qualifications. It is about the qualifications of the one who is sending you.

In the case of my foster daughter, we felt confident that, yes, God was sending her. So we began to pray, asking God what he wanted us to do. He laid it on our hearts to begin making bookmarks. And we made almost 4,000 bookmarks and raised that $5,000—most of it $1 at a time! She did go to Africa as a missionary that summer!

Sometimes when we look at a situation, it seems so overwhelming. We don't know what to do. And we give God an earful about what we *can't* do. But God says, "Don't tell me what you *can't* do. Tell me what you can do." Often it's not the so-called great things we can do for God that matter. God wants us to do small things with great faithfulness.

One of my favorite mottos is: Do what you can do and let God handle what you can't do.

It's never about the one who's going. It's about the one who's sending.

What is God calling you to do? What is the part you are supposed to play? Ask God to show you some small things you can begin to do, right now, to prepare for the task God has set out for you. Begin, today, to do those small things with great faithfulness. Do what you can do . . . and let God handle what you can't do. He's the Casting Director. Just play your part in the only Major Motion Picture that will last forever.

Steps to Freedom

Jesus said, "If you hold to my teaching, you are really my disciples. Then you will know the truth, and the truth will set you free."

John 8:31–32

The following steps to freedom with accompanying Scripture verses from the Bible are offered to you in the hope that you will know and believe the truth God has revealed in his Word. The whole Bible was written to reveal God to us in a special way so we could know who he is, what he is doing in the world, and how we can know him on a personal basis. The salvation God offers to all is the only way anyone can be set free from sin and death to live a life of true liberty by God's amazing grace through faith in his Son, the Lord Jesus Christ. "It is for freedom that Christ has set us free" (Gal. 5:1).

1. Believe that God exists.

In the beginning God created the heavens and the earth.

Genesis 1:1

The wrath of God is being revealed from heaven against all the godlessness and wickedness of men who suppress the truth by their wickedness, since what may be known about God is plain to them, because God has made it plain to them. For since the creation of the world God's invisible qualities—his eternal power and divine nature—have been clearly seen, being understood from what has been made, so that men are without excuse.

Romans 1:18–20

Now faith is being sure of what we hope for and certain of what we do not see. . . . And without faith it is impossible to please God, because anyone who comes to him must believe that he exists and that he rewards those who earnestly seek him.

Hebrews 11:1, 6

2. Know that God loves you.

The LORD is gracious and compassionate,
    slow to anger and rich in love.
The LORD is good to all;
    he has compassion on all he has made. . . .

The LORD is faithful to all his promises
    and loving toward all he has made.
The LORD upholds all those who fall
    and lifts up all who are bowed down.
The eyes of all look to you,
    and you give them their food at the proper time.

You open your hand
    and satisfy the desires of every living thing.

The LORD is righteous in all his ways
    and loving toward all he has made.
The LORD is near to all who call on him,
    to all who call on him in truth.
He fulfills the desires of those who fear him;
    he hears their cry and saves them.
The LORD watches over all who love him,
    but all the wicked he will destroy.

Psalm 145:8–9, 13–20

[God] causes his sun to rise on the evil and the good, and sends rain on the righteous and the unrighteous.

Matthew 5:45

For God so loved the world that he gave his one and only Son, that whoever believes in him shall not perish but have eternal life.

John 3:16

But God demonstrates his own love for us in this: While we were still sinners, Christ died for us.

Romans 5:8

3. Acknowledge and turn from your sin.

For all have sinned and fall short of the glory of God.

Romans 3:23

In the past God overlooked such ignorance, but now he commands all people everywhere to repent.

Acts 17:30

243

If we confess our sins, he is faithful and just and will forgive us our sins and purify us from all unrighteousness.

1 John 1:9

Therefore do not let sin reign in your mortal body so that you obey its evil desires. Do not offer the parts of your body to sin, as instruments of wickedness, but rather offer yourselves to God, as those who have been brought from death to life.

Romans 6:12–13

4. Accept that Jesus is the only way to God.

You diligently study the Scriptures because you think that by them you possess eternal life. These are the Scriptures that testify about me, yet you refuse to come to me to have life.

John 5:39–40

I am the way and the truth and the life. No one comes to the Father except through me.

John 14:6

Salvation is found in no one else, for there is no other name under heaven given to men by which we must be saved.

Acts 4:12

5. Realize that Jesus paid the penalty for your sins.

But he was pierced for our transgressions,
    he was crushed for our iniquities;
the punishment that brought us peace was upon him,
    and by his wounds we are healed.

244

We all, like sheep, have gone astray,
  each of us has turned to his own way;
and the LORD has laid on him
  the iniquity of us all.

Isaiah 53:5-6

For Christ died for sins once for all, the righteous for the unrighteous, to bring you to God. He was put to death in the body but made alive by the Spirit.

1 Peter 3:18

6. Receive Jesus as your Lord and Savior.

If you confess with your mouth, "Jesus is Lord," and believe in your heart that God raised him from the dead, you will be saved. For it is with your heart that you believe and are justified, and it is with your mouth that you confess and are saved. . . . for, "Everyone who calls on the name of the Lord will be saved."

Romans 10:9-10, 13

Yet to all who received him, to those who believed in his name, he gave the right to become children of God.

John 1:12

7. Follow God by doing his will every day for the rest of your life.

He has showed you, O man, what is good.
  And what does the LORD require of you?
To act justly and to love mercy
  and to walk humbly with your God.

Micah 6:8

245

Then [Jesus] said to them all: "If anyone would come after me, he must deny himself and take up his cross daily and follow me."

Luke 9:23

For it is by grace you have been saved, through faith—and this not from yourselves, it is the gift of God—not by works, so that no one can boast. For we are God's workmanship, created in Christ Jesus to do good works, which God prepared in advance for us to do.

Ephesians 2:8–10

One of them [the Pharisees], an expert in the law, tested him with this question: "Teacher, which is the greatest commandment in the Law?"

Jesus replied: "'Love the Lord your God with all your heart and with all your soul and with all your mind.' This is the first and greatest commandment. And the second is like it: 'Love your neighbor as yourself.' All the Law and the Prophets hang on these two commandments."

Matthew 22:36–40

Study Guide

Introduction: Are Your Problems Making You Crazy?
Verses to Memorize

> Pursue the things over which Christ presides. Don't shuffle along, eyes to the ground, absorbed with the things right in front of you. Look up, and be alert to what is going on around Christ—that's where the action is. See things from his perspective.

Colossians 3:1–2 Message

Passages for Digging Deeper

Psalm 31
Psalm 107
Lamentations 3:19–27
Romans 12:12
2 Corinthians 4:16–18

Recommended Movies to Watch

Anne of Green Gables, The King and I

How did the movie help you put your own problems into perspective?

Questions to Ponder

1. In what way do you live your life like it's a melodrama?

2. How can you make a conscious effort to turn your melodramas into mellow dramas?

Chapter 1: The Porcupine State of Mind

Verses to Memorize

Let us fix our eyes on Jesus, the author and perfecter of our faith, who for the joy set before him endured the cross, scorning its shame, and sat down at the right hand of the throne of God. Consider him who endured such opposition from sinful men, so that you will not grow weary and lose heart.

Hebrews 12:2–3

Passages for Digging Deeper

Matthew 18:21–35
Luke 6:32–42

Recommended Movie to Watch

Pollyanna

How did the movie help you put your own problems into perspective?

Questions to Ponder

1. Think of a specific time when you were in a Porcupine State of Mind. What were the results?

2. Who or what sends you into the Porcupine State of Mind most often?

3. On a scale of 1 to 10, how much of a porcupine are you?

4. What was your reaction to the Seventeenth-Century Nun's prayer? Take time to write it out and carefully ponder each line.

5. In what way does your sinful response to the sin of others trip you up?

6. Is there someone you need to forgive? Someone you need to be reconciled to? What steps do you need to take to make that happen?

Chapter 2: I Think I May Be Dying

Verse to Memorize

Since we have these promises, dear friends, let us purify
ourselves from everything that contaminates body and
spirit, perfecting holiness out of reverence for God.

                                                    2 Corinthians 7:1

Passages for Digging Deeper

Proverbs 17:22
1 Corinthians 6:19–20
2 Corinthians 7:1

Recommended Movie to Watch

Steel Magnolias

How did the movie help you put your own problems
into perspective?

Questions to Ponder

1. How would you rate your health on a scale of 1 to 10?

2. Is it possible that there's a mind-body connection involved in your various physical ailments? How so?

3. Could you relate to my description of living "sick and tired"? Describe your own experience of being sick and tired.

4. What is your response to the story of Naaman?

5. Are you availing yourself of the everyday miracles God has provided? In what way?

6. Ask the Holy Spirit to guide you in some specific steps you can take to improve your overall health and well-being. You might consider undertaking my 90-Day Renewal program, as set forth in *Becoming the Woman I Want to Be: 90 Days to Renew Your Spirit, Soul, and Body*.

Chapter 3: My Poor Nerves

Verses to Memorize

My son, pay attention to what I say;
    listen closely to my words.
Do not let them out of your sight,
    keep them within your heart;
for they are life to those who find them
    and health to a man's whole body.

Proverbs 4:20–22

Passages for Digging Deeper

Psalm 103:11–12
Isaiah 43:1–5
Philippians 4:4–9

Recommended Movies to Watch

Anne of Avonlea, Pride and Prejudice, The Secret Garden

How did the movie help you put your own problems into perspective?

Questions to Ponder

1. Is it easy for you to trust and obey . . . or do you
tend to doubt and disobey?

2. Go back and reread the meditation from *Come Away,
My Beloved*. Better yet, write it out. What is God
saying to you, personally, through its message?

3. Which of the "unworthy emotions" presents the
most significant stumbling block for you? Why do
you think that is?

4. Write out a Scripture verse that addresses that particular emotion. Memorize it and meditate upon
it often.

5. Make a list of things you cannot change. Now rip
it up or burn it. Determine not to spend any more
of your time and emotional energy focusing on
things you cannot change.

6. Make a list of things you can change. Write out a
strategy for making those changes over the next
thirty days. The next ninety days. The next year.

Chapter 4: I Can't Seem to Get a Moment's Peace

Verses to Memorize

May God himself, the God of peace, sanctify you through and through. May your whole spirit, soul and body be kept blameless at the coming of our Lord Jesus Christ. The one who calls you is faithful and he will do it.

1 Thessalonians 5:23–24

Passages for Digging Deeper

Reread the verses included in the chapter and be sure to write out what you learned from each.
Psalm 23

Recommended Movie to Watch

Sister Act

How did the movie help you put your own problems into perspective?

Questions to Ponder

1. Summarize the most significant insight you gained through meditation on the peace passages.

2. In the chapter, I painted two extremes: Christians who drive themselves to physical and emotional exhaustion trying to please God, and Christians who are content to sneak into heaven by the skin of their teeth. Where would you place yourself on a continuum between those two extremes? Explain your answer.

3. What are your Top 5 Mental Topics? List them below and note whether they bring peace or create turmoil:

Top 5 Mental Topics	Peace/Turmoil

4. What are the RATS in your life?

5. In what way have you been attracting them into your life?

6. What garbage do you need to get rid of, so that the rats will leave?

Chapter 5: Down and Out in Scorpionville

Verses to Memorize

Finally, be strong in the Lord and in his mighty power.
Put on the full armor of God so that you can take your
stand against the devil's schemes. For our struggle is not
against flesh and blood, but against the rulers, against
the authorities, against the powers of this dark world
and against the spiritual forces of evil in the heavenly
realms.

Ephesians 6:10–12

Passage for Digging Deeper

James 1

Recommended Movie to Watch

Out of Africa

How did the movie help you put your own problems
into perspective?

Questions to Ponder

1. Do you ever feel like God or the devil is picking on you? What makes you feel that way?

2. Have you ever asked, "If God loves me, why did he let this happen to me?" Describe the situation you were facing.

3. Are you now at a place where you have a better understanding of why it happened? If so, describe. If not, ask God for insight.

4. Did the example of the Scorpion House give you a better grasp of what's happening in this world? How so?

5. Is there something that keeps happening to you? What message do you need to "get" so that God can move on to the next lesson?

6. How can you convince your heart, once and for all, that God is good even when your circumstances are not?

7. Do you tend to learn your lessons the easy way or the hard way? How can you apply the effort to learn them the easy way, so that in the long run, your life will be much easier?

Chapter 6: How on Earth Am I Supposed to Find Time for God?

Verses to Memorize

And when you pray, do not keep on babbling like pagans, for they think they will be heard because of their many words. Do not be like them, for your Father knows what you need before you ask him.

This, then, is how you should pray:

Our Father in heaven,
hallowed be your name,
your kingdom come,
your will be done
on earth as it is in heaven.
Give us today our daily bread.

Matthew 6:7–11

My soul finds rest in God alone;
my salvation comes from him
He alone is my rock and my salvation;
he is my fortress, I will never be shaken.

Psalm 62:1–2

Passage for Digging Deeper

Begin reading in Mark 1 and read until you've gotten a good sense of Jesus's lifestyle.

Recommended Movies to Watch

The Gospel of John, Jesus of Nazareth

How did the movie help you put your own problems into perspective?

Questions to Ponder

1. How could investing time in spiritual disciplines actually save you time?

2. How did the analogy of prayer as "the gathering of gifts" alter your perspective? What changes do you need to make to your prayer life in response?

3. Create the physical space to meet with God. Set up a prayer room, or at least a prayer corner.

4. What rubble do you need to clear out of your life?

5. What is that "one room" in your life? What steps do you need to take to close the door on that room?

6. What changes do you need to make to become more of a disciple—one who learns by listening?

7. For at least the next week, set aside your prayer list. Instead, begin your prayer time with a blank notebook and pen. Ask God to show you what's on his prayer list.

Chapter 7: Okay, So You Had a Lousy Childhood

Verses to Memorize

Brothers, I do not consider myself yet to have taken hold of it. But one thing I do: Forgetting what is behind and straining toward what is ahead, I press on toward the goal to win the prize for which God has called me heavenward in Christ Jesus.

Philippians 3:13–14

Passage for Digging Deeper

Read Genesis 33

Recommended Movies to Watch

Ever After, Heidi, The Little Princess, any old Shirley Temple movie

How did the movie help you put your own problems into perspective?

Questions to Ponder

1. How would you describe your childhood in two sentences?

2. Do you rehearse old injuries? Is there someone you need to forgive or something you need to leave behind?

3. What destructive family patterns are still impacting your life?

4. What destructive family patterns are you passing on to your children?

5. In what ways are you still trapped in childish behaviors rooted in your childhood experience? Reread the list provided in the chapter to spark your thinking.

6. What is your "or else"? How can you defuse its power in your life—what truth from God's Word can counterbalance the lie?

Chapter 8: If You Think Your Marriage Is a Mess, Check This Out

Verse to Memorize

When they hurled their insults at him, he did not retaliate; when he suffered, he made no threats. Instead, he entrusted himself to him who judges justly.

1 Peter 2:23

Passage for Digging Deeper

Read Genesis 29 and 30

Recommended Movie to Watch

TNT Bible collection video series

How did the movie help you put your own problems into perspective?

Questions to Ponder

1. How did you react to the story of Leah?

2. Which sister do you identify with: Leah or Rachel? Why?

3. Do you agree or disagree with my assessment that Leah remained a porcupine to the end? (Yes, you are allowed to disagree!)

4. What "formula" have you been trying to follow in your own life?

5. Are you ready to admit that the formula has failed—that we walk by faith, not by formulas?

6. If you are married, what changes do you need to make in your attitude toward your spouse?

7. If you were previously married, was the Porcupine State of Mind a factor in the demise of your marriage?

Chapter 9: I Never Dreamed Parenting Would Be This Hard

Verses to Memorize

But from everlasting to everlasting
    the LORD's love is with those who fear him,
    and his righteousness with their children's
        children—with those who keep his covenant
    and remember to obey his precepts.

Psalm 103:17–18

Blessed is the man who fears the LORD,
    who finds great delight in his commands.
His children will be mighty in the land;
    the generation of the upright will be blessed.

Psalm 112:1–2

Passages for Digging Deeper

2 Samuel 13–15
Psalm 78
Psalm 103
Psalm 127

Recommended Movie to Watch

Documentary on *The Lost Boys of Sudan*

How did the movie help you put your own problems into perspective?

Questions to Ponder

1. Did the story of *The Lost Boys of Sudan* help you put your parenting problems into perspective? Why or why not?

2. Do you think most of the Christian parenting books you've read are realistic? Why or why not?

3. Can you think of people who clearly love the Lord, yet they have one or more children who walked away from the faith? Did you blame the parents?

4. Are you a First Generation Christian? If so, how were you impacted by the story I shared about my own family?

5. If you were raised in a Christian home, what was your response to my challenge to become a Mighty Musk Ox Warrior Princess?

Chapter 10: My Church Hurt My Feelings

Verses to Memorize

There should be no division in the body, but . . . its parts should have equal concern for each other. If one part suffers, every part suffers with it; if one part is honored, every part rejoices with it.

Now you are the body of Christ, and each one of you is a part of it.

1 Corinthians 12:25–27

Passages for Digging Deeper

1 Corinthians 5:9–13
1 Corinthians 12:1–31
Ephesians 3:7–21

Recommended Movie to Watch

Footloose

How did the movie help you put your own problems into perspective?

Questions to Ponder

1. Have you ever had an experience where you thought your pastor was "mean" but later realized he was simply telling you something you didn't want to hear? Describe.

2. What was your reaction to the statistic that fifteen hundred pastors leave the ministry every month?

3. Are you more of a joy—or a burden—to your pastor and your church? Give some evidence to support your answer. If you are really courageous, ask your church staff!

4. How has your church (or churches you were previously associated with) been impacted by The Real McCoy offenses?

5. Describe how the fallout affected you. Have you forgiven those involved?

273

6. Have you been guilty of pettiness—that is, obsessing over "My Church Hurt My Feelings" offenses? What changes do you need to make to be part of the solution at your church, rather than part of the problem?

Chapter 11: I'm Flat Broke

Verses to Memorize

But godliness with contentment is great gain. For we brought nothing into the world, and we can take nothing out of it. But if we have food and clothing, we will be content with that. People who want to get rich fall into temptation and a trap and into many foolish and harmful desires that plunge men into ruin and destruction. For the love of money is a root of all kinds of evil. Some people, eager for money, have wandered from the faith and pierced themselves with many griefs.

1 Timothy 6:6–10

Passages for Digging Deeper

Genesis 14:21–24
Deuteronomy 15:1–7
Psalm 37:21
Proverbs 3:9–10
Proverbs 6:6–8
Proverbs 21:5
Proverbs 22:7, 23–24, 27
Ecclesiastes 5:10–12
Romans 13:8

Recommended Movie to Watch

The Money Pit

How did the movie help you put your own problems into perspective?

Questions to Ponder

1. Do you currently tithe?

2. Do you agree with my conclusion that the reason we don't tithe is worry?

3. Calculate how much debt you currently have: _____ Why do you have that much debt, and do you believe it is pleasing to God?

4. Have you ever experienced that "sinking feeling" of being in over your head? How did it impact your spirit, soul, and body? Your relationships?

5. Do you have enough savings to last six months, if something catastrophic were to happen to your family? If not, how can you begin a savings plan?

6. Have financial problems ever impacted your marriage? How so?

7. What was your response to the closing story about the young boy's visit to the farm?

Chapter 12: The *Real* Major Motion Picture

Verse to Memorize

You did not choose me, but I chose you and appointed
you to go and bear fruit—fruit that will last.

John 15:16

Passage for Digging Deeper

Judges 6–8

Recommended Movies to Watch

*The Hiding Place, The Inn of the Sixth Happiness,
Chariots of Fire*

How did the movie help you put your own problems
into perspective?

Questions to Ponder

1. How can focusing on the Grand Drama help you turn your melodramas into mellow dramas?

2. Is there something God has called you to do, but since he hasn't given you all the answers up front, you refuse to take a step of faith?

3. Reread Ezekiel 22:30–31 and respond to its implications.

4. Do you believe E. M. Bounds was correct when he stated "God has chosen to limit His actions on this earth to those things done in direct response to believing prayer"? Why or why not?

5. How would your prayer life be different if you truly believed the advancement of God's kingdom depended upon our cooperating with him in prayer?

6. When has God "snookered" you?

7. What specific part do you believe God is calling you to play in the *Real* Major Motion Picture?

8. Do you agree with the statement "Foolish choices do not negate the call of God upon your life"? Why or why not?

9. What is the symbol of your disqualification? Will you allow God to work through it?

10. Name one thing you can do to begin fulfilling your part in the Grand Drama.

Notes

Introduction: Are Your Problems Making You Crazy?

1. Rick Warren, *The Purpose-Driven Life* (Grand Rapids: Zondervan, 2002), 41.

Chapter 1 The Porcupine State of Mind

1. When I use the term *enemy* I am not necessarily referring to Satan personally. He can only be in one place at a time, so the chance that he is personally attacking you at any given moment is quite remote. Instead, I am frequently referring to that legion of fallen angels who work to advance his agenda.

2. From an old photocopy someone gave me.

Chapter 2 I Think I May Be Dying

1. Online medical dictionary at www.cancerweb.com.

2. Audio by Dr. Pam Popper, copyrighted and distributed by NSA, Inc.

Chapter 3 My Poor Nerves

1. Frances Roberts, *Come Away, My Beloved* (Ojai, CA: King's Farspan, 1973), 92. A new hardcover gift edition with language updates is now available from Barbour Publishing (2002).

Chapter 4 I Can't Seem to Get a Moment's Peace

1. Oswald Chambers, *My Utmost for His Highest: An Updated Edition in Today's Language* (Grand Rapids: Discovery House Publishers, 1992), November 24.

2. William Backus and Marie Chapain, *Telling Yourself the Truth* (Minneapolis: Bethany, 1980), 59.

Chapter 5 Down and Out in Scorpionville

1. Oprah Winfrey, Oprah's column, *O* magazine, May 2004, 296.

2. Andrew Murray, *Humility* (Minneapolis: Bethany, 2001), 76.

Chapter 6 How on Earth Am I Supposed to Find Time for God?

1. Henri Nouwen, taken from a Lenten pamphlet, "From Fear to Love," http://www.btc-bci.com/~jneiman/Columns/living_as_god.htm or http://marcsmessages.typepad.com/mm/2004/03/exploring_the_c.html.

2. I first read this concept in a devotional, *From Fear to Love*, based on the writings of Henri Nouwen.

Chapter 10 My Church Hurt My Feelings

1. Philip Yancey, *What's So Amazing about Grace?* (Grand Rapids: Zondervan, 1997), 254.

2. Ibid.

3. Ibid., 259.

4. Ibid., 262.

5. Ibid., 266.

6. Ibid., 267.

Chapter 11 I'm Flat Broke

1. Lynn Brezosky, "Pay Sent Home Makes Big Difference," *San Diego Union-Tribune*, May 31, 2004, A21.

2. Statistics from a sermon by Dr. Gary Kinnaman, Word of Grace Church, www.wordofgrace.org.

3. John C. Murray, American Bankruptcy Institute, Bankruptcy Facts 2003, www.ABIworld.org.

4. Survey statistic quoted in Victor M. Parachin, "Money Conflicts," *Vibrant Life* (January 1,1999), http://static.highbeam.com/v/vibrantlife/january011999/moneyconflict/.

5. Phone interview with Steve Moore of Crown Financial Ministries (www.crown.org), and statistics from the Bureau of Labor Statistics (www.bls.gov).

Chapter 12 The *Real* Major Motion Picture

1. If you are doing this as part of a group, you can debate among yourselves whether God simply picked those who he knew in advance would pick him; but you must promise to debate it nicely. Christians have argued over this issue for centuries, and sincere people sincerely disagree. We can all agree that God picks us for a purpose!

2. E. M. Bounds, *E. M. Bounds on Prayer* (New Kensington, PA: Whitaker House, 1997), 342.

Donna Partow is one of America's most popular Christian speakers and writers. Based in Arizona, she travels worldwide to communicate the transforming power of God. Her books have sold more than half a million copies and have been translated in many languages, and her best sellers include *Becoming a Vessel God Can Use* and *Becoming the Woman I Want to Be*. Donna invites readers and speaking events planners to visit her popular website at www.donnapartow.com.

A Beautiful Pot From the Miry Clay

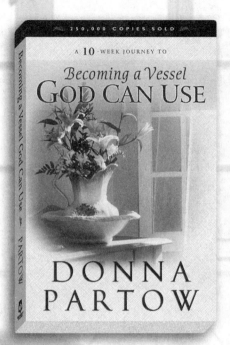

Do you ever wonder where you fit in to God's grand plan? Do you ever wonder if there really is a place for you? God accomplishes extraordinary things through ordinary people—imperfections and all. *Becoming a Vessel God Can Use* is a ten-week journey that offers hope, laughter, and transformation to women who long to discover new confidence and significance.

Becoming a Vessel God Can Use
by Donna Partow

BETHANYHOUSE

Four Studies Written *for* Women

WRITTEN IN DONNA'S CANDID voice, this twelve session Bible study series will draw you into closer fellowship with God as you study the Bible, ponder its message, and apply it to your life.

"Donna's writing brings renewed hope and revives your walk with God."
—PAM FARREL-author of *Woman of Influence*

EXTRACTING THE PRECIOUS FROM:

- *2 Corinthians*
- *Isaiah*
- *Galatians*
- *Nehemiah*

by Donna Partow with Lin Johnson

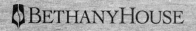

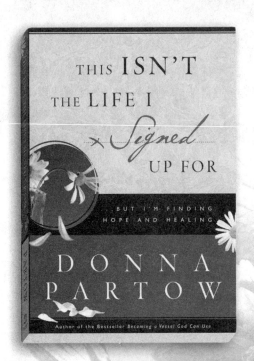

Finding Hope & Healing Through Life's Hard Times

"Hey, God, this isn't the life I signed up for!" No one signs up for the challenges of life, but in the real world, heartache is inevitable. As Donna tells stories from her own life, you'll recognize your life, your struggles, and broken dreams. Donna says, "If God can breathe new life into my weary heart and soul, there's hope for everyone!"

This Isn't the Life I Signed Up For
by Donna Partow

BETHANYHOUSE